The Anatomy of
Life & Energy
in Agriculture

Third Edition

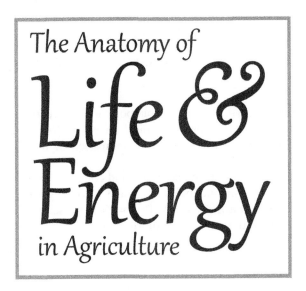

The Anatomy of Life & Energy in Agriculture

Third Edition

Dr. Arden B. Andersen

Acres U.S.A.
Greeley, Colorado

The Anatomy of Life & Energy in Agriculture

Copyright © 1989, 2011, 2014, 2021 by Arden B. Andersen

Acres U.S.A.
P.O. Box 1690
Greeley, Colorado 80631 U.S.A.
(970) 392-4464 • (800) 355-5313 U.S./Canada
info@acresusa.com • www.acresusa.com

Printed in the United States of America

Publisher's Cataloging-in-Publication

Andersen, Arden B. 1958-
    The anatomy of life and energy in agriculture / Arden B. Andersen. Greeley, CO: ACRES U.S.A., 2014.
        xiv, 121pp., 23cm.
        3rd edition.
        Includes index, tables, and photos
        ISBN 978-1-60173-075-6 (trade)
        1. Alternative agriculture. 2. Sustainable agriculture. 3. Agricultural ecology. 4. Refractometers. I. Andersen, Arden B., 1958– II. Title

S494.5 .A53   2014
631.584

Dedication & Thanks

This book is dedicated to the ascension of mankind, to those who choose to eat to *live* over mere survival or existence, to those who wish to experience the joy of eating the truly high-quality food God intended for us to enjoy, to those who choose to coexist with planet Earth rather than co-destruct, and, most of all, to the greatest miracles of all, *the children*, both those present and those yet unborn. One of the greatest expressions of our love is to provide them with healthy, healthful, *life*-giving food in accordance to God's divine blueprint. A healthy, vibrant, happy child is indeed the manifestation of love.

In addition, I convey my love and deepest appreciation to my father for the many hours of exchanging ideas and practical advice; to my mother for her patience and enthusiasm; to my many friends for their support, enthusiasm, and insightful evaluations — especially Cynthia Dunster, Ted and Rose Baroody, Gene and Margie Logue, Asparita, and Jackie Woods. Special thanks go to Christopher D. Walters, whose editorial skills conferred upon this book a professional literary tone it otherwise would not have enjoyed.

Finally, I give my thanks, respect, and deepest appreciation to the person who conveyed to me the basic foundation of my development in this work and posed the many initial challenges which have fueled my curiosity. I shall never forget his favorite statement, "See what you look at." He was Dr. Carey Reams.

Contents

For the Record

I first met Arden Andersen a few years ago at an Acres U.S.A. conference. We had lunch together, and he outlined his philosophy of farming for me. I was impressed by Arden's knowledge of the living soil. I suggested that as a research project he obtain from Bartington Instrument Company in Oxford, England, a magnetic susceptibility meter to study the paramagnetic properties of soil. He did so and in short time demonstrated that the cgs (centimeters/grams/per second) reading of the soil varies over time (twenty-four-hour cycle). The same phenomenon of course, happens to rock from which soil derives.

Unlike the magnetic susceptibility meter, which we understand, Arden also utilizes, and gets results, with that mysterious box we call a *radionics* instrument. Arden calls it an *electronic scanner*, which in my opinion is a better term for it than either radionics or the *eloptic energy* term used by Galen Hieronymus. Incidentally, there are almost two hundred terms used internationally for the energy measured by Andersen.

Radionics was invented by Albert Abrams at the turn of the century. The best known developers in the United States have been Galen Hieronymus and Pete Kelly. As in all new discoveries, more than one person has been involved. Surely, no man is an island unto himself. In the final analysis, however — whatever the instrument ends up being called — it should be admitted that it measures a series of electronic *tuned circuits* hooked to an *antenna* at one end and an *oscillator* (the human body) at the other end. How do I know? Because Arden let me take his instrument apart, which vouches for his intellectual honesty. The tuned circuit and antenna was invented, as is well documented in patents, by Nikola Tesla, so he is the real father of the radionics instrument in its present state as marketed in the U.S.A.

I believe that utilized by a trained and sensitive operator, this instrument works. The key words are *sensitive operator*, for not everyone can run the 440 in record time. Some will do better than others. In my opinion, the three pentode-tuned circuits serve as an impedance matching device between the antenna (soil in the input well) and the oscillator (the human being).

Regardless of whether or not one believes in the electronic scanner instrument, Arden's book is a marvelous treatise on how to prepare the soil. His philosophy is summarized in one phrase quoted from this well-written book, "chlorophyll energy over wires."

He demonstrated in detail the fallacy of the agribusiness method of nurturing soil and put a "hammerlock" on the insane recommendations coming out of many university experiment stations and government laboratories.

The chemistry that Arden outlines is not a quick-fix-drug-for-soil chemistry, but a gentle, love-and-feed-for-soil chemistry, based on solid biochemical and biophysical processes.

I recommend that gardeners and farmers read the first four chapters carefully. They outline in detail the difference between deadly slow-kill agribusiness farming and farming as it should be. Thank you, Arden, for a well-written and informative book — a book for all who love country and soil and strive to keep farming a partnership with God.

Philip S. Callahan, PhD
Gainesville, Florida, 1989

Foreword

The year is 2014. We are printing the third edition of this book thanks to Fred Walters and Acres U.S.A. As I have reviewed this book I find there are certainly items that need updating regarding current events. At the same time I noted that most items or issues of food quality, environmental pollution, human health, chronic disease, chemical use, and soil destruction have only declined further. The basic science of nature has not changed a bit. It has actually been solidified further having stood the test of time. On the good side, soil erosion has declined, according to the USDA Natural Resources Conservation Service (NRCS), from 3.06 billion tons per year in 1982 to 1.725 billion tons per year in 2007. We also farm fewer acres now than we did in 1982, but the per-acre soil loss has declined from 7.24 tons per acre to 4.87 tons per acre. We still have a ways to go in stopping the loss of topsoil.[1]

We have improved our trade balance for beef from 1985, and have a net positive trade balance for agricultural products ($115.8 billion exported: $81.9 billion imported in 2010).[2]

This is a bit misleading with regards to food since included in these figures are cotton, wool, and tobacco. The point to make is

---

[1] "Soil Erosion on Cropland 2007," USDA Natural Resources Conservation Services, 2007, http://www.nrcs.usda.gov/wps/portal/nrcs/detail/national/technical/nra/nri/?cid=stelprdb1041887.

[2] See http://www.census.gov/compendia/statab/cats/agriculture/agricultural_exports_and_imports.html.

that the United States is a long way from "feeding the world." In fact, the genetically engineered corn and soybeans and glyphosate-laden cereal grains, corn, and soybeans contribute more to the demise of the world population than its survival. We still have a lot of work to do, but the grassroots movement in biological agriculture is strong and much larger than in 1989 when the first edition of this book was published. We do have better products, better technologies, better understanding of the workings of nature, and many more excellent groups as part of the quest. Certainly, we do have a lot of pushback from the chemical company–funded universities and their mouthpieces. No matter, the grassroots movement and truth will inevitably prevail.

So, too, have I advanced since 1989. I now have a medical degree and practice, a master's of science in public health and board certification, and many years under my belt as a flight doc and crop consultant. I have traveled extensively and found that the same problems exist in other countries as they do in the United States. I was particularly disappointed upon a recent trip to New Zealand because my and most Americans' perception of New Zealand is that it is the land of green, clean and pristine. It probably was thirty years ago. Today it is adapting American farm destruction technology, perhaps faster than any other country, taking on the American feedlot dairy model complete with genetically modified feed, animal health problems, and decline in milk quality. New Zealand seems determined to match the Dutch in polluting their waterways with nitrogen runoff. The minister for the environment in January 2013 stated that over half of all New Zealand waterways are now unsafe for swimming. "Why is this happening?" one may ask. Just follow the money from the chemical and biotech industry to the university departments to the political campaign funds to the chemical sales reps and the vets who make much of their money selling drugs! Fortunately, there is a very strong grassroots movement afoot in New Zealand proving that not only can farmers sequester carbon, they can also regenerate the soils, environment, and the food chain with appropriate nutritional farm management at greater profit per acre/hectare than can the drug and chemical crowd. Peter Floyd of eCOGENT has shown with five years of farm financial data, the higher the pasture Brix reading the greater the per acre/hectare profit.

I have kept most of the original version of this book intact because this information is as relevant today as ever. Read on and enjoy. Thank you for your patronage.

◆

We have the fortune of inhabiting a beautiful miracle of nature. Where else can one find the ideal circumstances for sustaining life? Unfortunately, our planet is dying. It is becoming less and less fit to sustain life. The fertile soils are disappearing. The fresh, clean waters are becoming polluted and poisoned. Vast forests are dying or being stripped. People and animals are dying of widespread starvation, and many are dying due to malnutrition even though their stomachs are full. The food is deficient because the soil is deficient.

Agricultural practices prevalent for the past hundred years are based upon invalid theory by the simple fact that they do not work. If they were valid, we would not have the polluted streams, rivers, underground aquifers, lakes, soils, foods, animals, and human beings. According to the May 3, 1985, issue of *Minnesota Land Magazine*, the United States has lost approximately half of its topsoil in the last hundred years. The 2010 National Resources Inventory Summary Report estimates that the United States is losing 1.72 billion tons of soils on crop lands per year. All for what? Facts are facts. They do not change. Theories can be changed and so can the destruction of our environment. That is a fact. Have you ever wondered why some of the most deadly chemicals were invented? Try *agriculture*. How much of industry's pollution is a result of producing something for agriculture? And what about energy consumption? The agricultural industry is the second-largest consumer of energy in the country. Where have we placed our priorities? When soil degenerates, the growing plants degenerate and the consumers degenerate. This in turn creates a demand for the production and sale of products to combat the symptoms degenerate soil creates. There are products to fumigate the soil for insects and diseases, chemicals for weeds, and finally chemicals for doctors to give sick consumers to cover up new maladies and diseases. Are short-term profits worth long-term bankruptcy? The September 27, 1984, issue of *New Scientist* stated that between 1960 and 1979 Czech farmers tripled their fertilizer use. Yet crop yields increased by only 52 percent. The soil was damaged, and now yields are diminishing with no decrease in fertilizer usage. The United States, considered the world leader in agricultural technology, exported this technology to the Czech Republic. How humane.

Consider a fact closer to home. According to the *Statistical Abstract of the U.S. 1985*, 105th edition, U.S. Department of Commerce, Bureau of the Census, page 668, the U.S. exported 312 million pounds of beef but *imported* 1,931 billion pounds of beef, or over six times what was exported that year.[1] The government then turns around and claims that we have surpluses because the American farmer is overproducing. The irony of it all is that people who are profiting financially are as sick as or sicker than anyone else. Their profits can't buy health.

The mass media, the FDA, and the National Cancer Institute would like the public to believe that human health and longevity has improved over the past thirty-five years, even though cancer is a $60 billion business annually, and growing.

According to the National Center for Health Statistics, over the thirty-three-year period between 1975 and 2008 there was no significant increase in overall survival rates for cancer patients.[2] One in every three Americans is ill with cancer versus one in seven thirty years ago. Health in America has been and is declining, and this decline directly parallels agriculture. Revitalize the health of the soils and crops will be revitalized. As a consequence they will become nutritionally healthful for consumers.

There is a way out and up. This book outlines the beginning steps one can take to make this ascension. Good health is no accident. It is a natural phenomenon. The first place to begin is with education. You must know the facts. Seek and you shall find. Enjoy your journey. Truth is ever simple. Falsity is ever complex.

---

[1] Per the *2012 Statistical Abstract of the United States*, the United States in 2010 exported 6.37 million metric tons of beef, pork, lamb, and poultry meat, while it imported 1.35 million metric tons of the same.

[2] "Health, United States, 2012," National Center for Health Statistics, 2013, http://www.cdc.gov/nchs/data/hus/hus12.pdf#043.

Chapter 1

Life & Energy

I prefer to define life as love. In love there is progression. It is very difficult to progress mentally, emotionally, or spiritually if one is not in the best possible health physically. Life should be a celebration. Growing your own food should be a celebration. After all, it should be teeming with life. Since we are what we eat, our body is only as vital as the food we eat.

The basis of life is God. (If this infringes upon your belief system, insert Creator, Universal Life Force, or whatever you are comfortable with.) God supplies the life force energy; everything is energy, whether it be thought, soil, air, water, or some chemical. What makes each thing different is the energy pattern and frequency at which it resonates. Some patterns and frequencies are detrimental to biological life and some are beneficial. Our goal is to minimize the detrimental and maximize the beneficial.

Most people are familiar with electrical energy at least to the degree that they understand AC/DC current. It enables us to use electrical appliances such as lights and computers and can cause great bodily harm if misused. This energy is only a very special case of the universal energy I am referring to; in fact, the electrical energy we use every day is actually quite primitive and even more primitively and inefficiently generated. According to Professor Shirrichi Seike, director of the Gravity Research Laboratory in Chime, Japan, there are 8.8×10^{13} volts per centimeter in the ether, tachyon-field, or energy bubble in which we live. This is a part of the life energy provided for us free of charge. Nikola Tesla proved and demonstrated in the late 1890s that this energy could be tapped to operate conventional electrical machines and could also be transmitted around the world without wires with a loss of less than one-half of 1 percent. In 1931, Tesla invented and engineered an energy converter which he combined with an electric motor, installed it in a Pierce Arrow automobile, and performance-tested it. The car performed comparably to gasoline powered autos and cruised at 90 mph, totally without pollution or fuel expense.

Dr. Henry Moray invented a free energy convertor and applied for a patent on July 13, 1931, only to have it rejected because the patent office did not understand its supposedly impossible principle of operation.

In 1948 Dr. Wilhelm Reich coupled a 0.5 volt exciter dynamo with an orgone energy accumulator to supply a 25 volt motor with a permanent energy supply. "Orgone" is the term Wilhelm Reich gave to the life force energy of the ether, or atmosphere. It is the primordial, mass-free energy out of which all matter manifests. More recently in free energy generation came the Permanent Magnet Motor, U.S. No. 4,151,432, April 24, 1979; the Kieninger N-Machine and the De Palma "Sunburst" N-Machine; and the Transistorized and Mobius Coils.

What does this have to do with growing plants or gardening? Everything. The same energy that Tesla, Moray, and Reich tapped to produce conventional energy is what plants and animals, including humans, live on.

We are usually taught that life on planet Earth is directly or indirectly dependent on sunshine. The life cycle is typically depicted as starting with sunlight, water, and carbon dioxide, plus some essential nutrients. Matter is produced in the form of organisms called plants, which contain chlorophyll. Plants are then consumed by animals for food and sometimes the animals are consumed for food by other animals. This food is digested by the consumer and the unusable portion is returned to the earth to be recycled. Many statistics and so-called factual conclusions have arisen from this hypothesis. Such statements as, "It takes a given number of heat units to mature a crop" (heat units are defined as time in relation to temperature above a certain minimum temperature), or "plants must have sunlight to undergo photosynthesis." The dominant assertion is that life depends upon those things we can or choose to observe via our five senses, which we only use within an arbitrarily defined limit. Simply speaking, these conclusions are not incorrect. They just do not explain what is really happening in the fabulous wonders of nature.

Dr. T. Galen Hieronymus showed decades ago that plants did not necessarily need sunlight to grow normally. Dr. Hieronymus coined the term *eloptic energy*. He essentially observed and worked with the same energy that Reich termed orgone energy. The following is his account:

CHLOROPHYLL ENERGY OVER WIRES

About 1930, I decided to try an experiment of conducting chlorophyll energy over wires. I had been conducting eloptic energy over long distance via wire.

A wood platform was installed on the south side of the house about six feet above ground. Later experiments indicated that the platform must be at least six feet above ground in order to get the desired potential of energy which increases with distance above ground.

Having some wooden cigar boxes available, I cut boxes apart and cut pieces and made eight boxes that were two inches by two inches by four inches, although any size boxes will work.

Aluminum foil was placed on the bottom of seven boxes inside so as to be in contact with the soil. Similar pieces of foil were placed on the underside of the lid of each box. Wires were connected to each piece of foil, the wires from the lids were extended to the sun plates, the wires from the bottom foils were connected to the water pipe and thus grounded.

Refer to figure 1 which shows a side view of the installation.

Seven plates were placed on the platform so as to pick up energy from the sun and wire was connected to each plate and extended down into the basement, each box, having the top foil plate connected via wire to a plate out on the platform in the sunlight. The eighth box had no connection to the outside, it being the control.

The plates placed on the platform were all different in size. The smallest was two inches by four inches, the next four inches by eight inches, the largest was about eight inches by ten inches, and one plate was copper screen wire.

Some soil was screened and a half inch of it placed in each box. Oat seeds were selected, all of uniform size, and planted in two rows of five seeds spaced in each row, then a half inch of dirt was placed on top in the box. The same amount of water was added to each box as needed from day to day.

All of the seeds sprouted about the same time. Then we noticed that there was no chlorophyll in the ten plants in the control box. All of the boxes connected to outside plates had plants with much chlorophyll.

We were quite surprised to note that the plants in boxes with large outside plates seemed to look as if they had been subjected to heat. Apparently, the large outside plates were bringing in an excess of energy compared with the effect of the small size outside plates.

Very soon the plants grew too tall for the small amount of head room in the boxes, so each box was equipped with a spacer to raise the top of each lid up about three-fourths of an inch.

The boxes were placed on a shelf in the end of the basement where there was little light, with no windows at the end. Also, the shelf was kept dark by a board placed in front and another on top to exclude all light. The plants were dark all of the time except when they were examined by flashlight.

A friend tried to duplicate the experiment but did not follow all instructions. Their basement was only about three feet from basement floor to ground level outside. Thus they did not have the potential difference between outside collector and inside boxes and the experiment was a failure. Also, there was a window nearby that let much light into where the boxes were placed.

Anyone who expects to duplicate an experiment should be sure they know all the factors and that they follow the instructions exactly without any substitution or change. And as to changes, if you are trying to get a special result and are trying out several methods or ideas, one of the cardinal points to doing good work is to make just *one* change at a time. Then you know just what the results are. If you make two changes and the result is failure, you do not know but that one of the changes may have been all right.

Figure 1

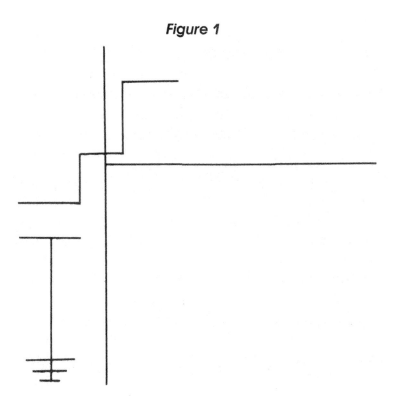

Dr. Wilhelm Reich also revealed that plants can grow without direct light by growing normal healthy plants inside his orgone accumulator.

Hans Nieper, MD, an internist at the Paracelsus Silbersee Hospital in Hanover, Germany, is internationally renowned for his work in cancerous diseases, multiple sclerosis, mineral and electrolyte metabolism, aging, and the prevention of cardiac infarction, as well as his medical association activities, including gravity field energy research. According to Dr. Nieper, every biologically active cell, including a human cell, represents a housing covered on all sides by an electrically charged membrane with double contortions. This is necessary for the conversion of orgone energy into heat.

An article from the University of New York at Buffalo that appeared in *Science*, August 3, 1984, stated, "The nerve there is an electric shunt between the central axon fiber and the myelin, which is a multilayer wrapping of a double-contoured leaf of a cell membrane system." This finding means in essence that our nerves own a pure "Tesla function" and seem to extract a major part of their effector energy from space.

In over sixty years of agricultural research, Dr. Carey Reams showed that plants accumulate more energy (mass) than can possibly be accounted for from fertilizer and water, thus his conclusion that only about 20 percent of the energy is obtained from the soil, while about 80 percent is obtained from the air. This principle is compatible with the alkaline-to-acid ratio of nutrients in the human body. For optimum health, it is estimated that there needs to be 80 percent alkaline elements and 20 percent acidic elements.

H. H. Robertson, DVM, conducted studies with chickens that proved the chickens produced or expelled more calcium than could be accounted for in their diet, thus the conclusion that the balance is transmuted via, from, or with the air, orgone energy.

Does all of this energy information make you turn up your nose, elicit a doubt, or cause outright disbelief? Or does it tug at your mind and elicit curiosity or outright enthusiasm? We are peeking into that actual, real life miracle of which we are all a part and which is part of us all: *Creation*. Prevailing science, especially agricultural science in this case, gives the impression that nature is primitive or at least less intelligent than man. Consequently, man can outsmart, overpower, and manipulate to his desires the creation of which he is a part. He boasts of increased production, insect and disease eradication, hybridization, specialization, and every other "-ization" that pops up. But nature doesn't live by the law of greed. Man in his greed for power and dominance over his environment has ensured an eventual day of reckoning. His claims of increased production mock the level of quality that has been sacrificed and the production levels that can be attained. In 1851, the Reverend John L. Blake wrote in *The Farmer's Everyday Book* about yields of 800 bushels of potatoes per acre on four acres and 100 bushels of corn per acre on forty acres with yields as high as 145 and 180 bushels per acre on three- and five-acre fields. How large was a four-acre field in 1851, when there were no tractors, commercial fertilizers, or chemicals?

According to the government's own figures, this country has lost about one-half of its topsoil since the turn of the twentieth century. Supposedly this has been the century of greatest technological advancement, yet the deprivation, degradation, destruction, and contamination of this planet worsens every day. Sympathizers contend that it cannot be blamed on technology, for the intensity of farming has simply increased due to demand. Well, demand isn't going to decrease because the world population isn't going to decrease — quite the contrary. I agree, however, that technology is not the culprit, for true technology provides mankind with free, unpolluting energy to light his lights, power his machines, heat his homes, propel his transportation systems, and, most importantly, provide him with food that doesn't rot, carry contaminates, or require rescue chemistry for disease, insect, and pest control.

Farming for the most part has actually become mining. The true farmer and caretaker of the land produces better and better crops, and leaves the soil in better shape each year while needing fewer inputs.

The life cycle of nature is an expanding spiral. At the base of this spiral is the soil.

Chapter 2

Progressive Biological Life

Soil is alive. It more than simply supports life. Living soil is healthy and healthful. It allows for the growth and development of healthy, healthful plants — plants that fulfill the nutritional needs of animals and people. Dead soil is dirt. It does not produce healthy animals and people. It does not produce healthy vegetation. It erodes. It compacts. It clods. It no longer carries an adequate electromagnetic charge.

This charge is the manifestation of the life force in the soil. It is a result of biological balance. As this balance is disturbed, the ability of the soil to sustain the charge diminishes. If the biological balance is disrupted by the misapplication of mineral elements, this causes electrical chaos, which leads to the degeneration of biologically active carbon. Finally, if mismanagement continues, degradation overwhelms regeneration, producing symptoms of erosion, compaction, pest infestations, and plant diseases. This phenomenon is not exclusive to this decade. An article by Rex Beach published in the June 1936 issue of *Cosmopolitan* indicates that this degradation started several decades ago.

The article, titled "Modern Miracle Men," discussed the first serious research in the field of human illness as it relates to soil fertility. It quoted Charles Northern, MD, an Alabama physician who specialized in stomach diseases and nutritional disorders. He was the first to assert that soil-building is the basis of food-building, which is the basis of human-building. "Bear in mind," wrote Dr. Northern, "that minerals are vital to human metabolism and health — and that no plant or animal can appropriate to itself any mineral which is not present in the soil upon which it feeds." Dr. Northern stated that the majority of our soils do not contain adequate minerals to produce healthful foodstuffs. Soil analyses, he pointed out, only reflect the content of the samples. He found that foods varied enormously in mineral content. Some of them weren't worth eating. Foods he tested varied in mineral content from more than six times the standards to nothing. He found that dietary mineral deficiencies caused everything from disrupted heartbeat to mental illness, and then traced these deficiencies back to the soil. He also proved that after reestablishing the mineral balance in the soil, plants were bigger, more vigorous, faster growing, disease and insect free, and contained minerals proportionate to those in the soil. He was able to double and redouble the mineral content of fruits and vegetables, increase the mineral levels of milk and eggs and improve the shelf life of all foodstuffs simply by remineralizing the soil.

He was also able to successfully treat human disease by simply injecting highly mineralized foods into their diets. Dr. Northern stated, "Healthy plants mean healthy people. We can't raise a strong race on a weak soil." He encouraged the public to demand highly mineralized food to create the supply. "It is simpler to cure sick soils than sick people. Which shall we choose?"

Unfortunately, the public was timid then. There was more profit in drugs and farm chemicals than in mineralization. The public is less timid now, but the basics of food production are unchanged.

The only difference between 1989 and 1936 (when that article was written) is that there have been fifty years of further mining and polluting of the soil. Unfortunately, the trend in declining nutrient value of our food has continued through 2014. The widespread use of glyphosate has further demineralized crops via chelating them out. Plant pathologist Dr. Don Huber in his presentations points out numerous studies showing crop mineral levels to be significantly lower where glyphosate has been applied compared to where it has not been applied.

It is not necessary to be a chemist to understand these principles and successfully apply them. One needs only determination to have better health. It helps to become familiar with the terms of the trade, so it is recommended, then, that the reader commit to memory the major chemical symbols and product names. The most commonly cited elements of soil chemistry are carbon (C), hydrogen (H), oxygen (O), calcium (Ca), potassium (K) (usually called potash), iron (Fe), magnesium (Mg), nitrogen (N), phosphorus (P), sulfur (S), manganese (Mn), boron (B), zinc (Zn), copper (Cu), molybdenum (Mo), chlorine (Cl), cobalt (Co), and selenium (Se). These are not the only elements found in healthy soil, but they are a good list to begin with.

Freeing the flow of the magnetic field in the soil is basic to any soil fertility program. Balancing the minerals is the key to freeing the magnetic field. A compass verifies the existence of this magnetic field but does not, however, measure the field strength. The field strength varies by latitude. If you grow a variety of corn in Alaska in two months and take the same variety of corn to Mexico, it will take six to eight months for it to grow. This is due to the concentration of the magnetic field, assuming that the soil fertility is equal in both locations. A rule to remember is that plants, animals, and humans all live on energy, the energy released by the interaction of elements. This is the fuel that powers life processes.

To succeed we need a plan, materials, and some guidelines. Two rules have already been mentioned: 80 percent of a plant comes from the air and 20 percent from the soil; plants grow on the energy released from the interaction of nutrients. In addition: Nature always follows the lines of least resistance; like attracts like even though opposite charges attract; all nutrients should enter the plant in the phosphate form; if a nutrient is soluble it does not necessarily mean it is available to the plant; plant growth is not limited by time, only energy; some nutrient compounds produce growth, some nutrient compounds produce fruit; and see what you look at!

Next come the building materials. First and foremost is calcium. Calcium determines the volume of crop and is the major element against which other nutrients react to release energy. It is a major constituent in all cell membranes. It is nature's detoxifier, meaning it has a great capacity for neutralizing toxicities either via transmutation or chemical/physical bonding. Ideally (since it is the foundation element upon which all else is built), when calcium is sufficiently present, the biological entity, whether it be a single cell, a plant, an animal or human, is able to discard toxins readily and does not have any magnetic attraction for environmental toxins such as pesticides, herbicides, or drugs. In addition, there will be sufficient energy to actually transmute the toxins in to alternate, harmless substances. And since calcium is the foundation element for all biological life, it is needed continuously. It is needed for all growth, whether in plants, foliage, or fruit.

It is usually argued that most of the calcium is taken into the plant early in the growing season and very little late in the season. This is correct, but the reason is that the plant does not have a great enough magnetic attraction late in the season. This is due to insufficient nutrition early in the growing season, which is easily verified by electronic scanner evaluation or refractometer readings (which will be discussed in Chapter 6). Calcium is the most neglected nutrient in most current fertilization programs, and this neglect is the primary cause of soil demise. The reason calcium is overlooked centers on the lack of knowledge about pH. It is taught that the soil pH relates directly to the need for liming, which is the term given to the application of a dry calcium compound or product. People with important-sounding titles and degrees persuade farmers who do not know the technical jargon that the calcium requirements of the soil are determined by its pH. Since they seem to know what they are saying, their audience swallows it hook, line, and sinker. It is almost as pertinent to say that the volume of your automobile's engine coolant is determined by its temperature. Hardly. Under normal conditions, the thermostat determines the temperature. The coolant volume is determined by how much was originally put in minus how much was taken out, leaked out, or somehow evaporated.

The pH is technically the negative logarithm of the hydrogen ion concentration. Hydrogen is the element, in this case the ion, whose concentration is the standard by which solutions, elements, compounds, etc., are classified as to their acidity or alkalinity. Any competent professional chemist will explain that the pH of a solution is not a volumetric measurement. It is a relative state of acidity or alkalinity. Two examples come to mind. In the western United States the soil pH is often above eight, yet the available and sometimes the total calcium content is very low and lime or calcium is added. In many southern soils that are high in bauxite, the soil pH often runs below six, yet there may be plenty of calcium available. Pure distilled water has a pH of about 6.8 to 7.0, yet there is no calcium present. I will let the reader contemplate the reasons for the misuse of the concept, but it is interesting to remember that calcium lime is one of the least expensive fertilizers or plant foods one can purchase. In most parts of the country, high-calcium lime costs about $20-plus per ton. The common acid fertilizers range from $120 to $300 per ton. Lime is often applied one year out of several and the cost is amortized over these years while the acid fertilizers are applied seasonably. At lower the calcium levels, which we have in America today, greater amounts of acid fertilizers must be applied to achieve a given volume. The catch is that volume achieved via this practice is not synonymous with quality, as proven by the current use of chemicals for insect and disease control. There is obviously more room for profit margin in a $120-per-ton fertilizer than a $20-per-ton fertilizer, especially when the $120 fertilizer results in the follow-up with herbicides and pesticides to even achieve a crop, then further follow-up with preservatives to keep the crop from rotting; further follow-up with animal and human dietary supplementation with the nutrients which should have been in the food and further follow-up with health care needed for the nutritionally deficient animals and people. People and animals are starving to death on full stomachs.

Drs. Northern and Reams, as well as the famous University of Missouri soil scientist Dr. William A. Albrecht, all insisted that calcium was the main staple nutrient for truly healthy plants and animals. These men proved beyond any doubt this principle, yet their teachings even today are not universally adopted and are often scorned.

Calcium can be obtained from several sources. The following is a listing of commonly available forms:

- Calcium carbonate (AG lime, hi-cal lime), $CaCO_3$
- Calcium oxide (dehydrated lime), CaO
- Calcium sulfate (gypsum), $CaSO_4$
- Calcium hydroxide (slake lime, hot lime, hydrated lime), $Ca(OH)$
- Arrogonite (ground seashells from Bermuda)
- Soft rock phosphate
- Paper mill lime (often contaminated, avoid)
- Sugar beet lime (often contaminated, be cautious or avoid)
- Basic slag (beware of contaminants, i.e., heavy metal)
- Dolomite lime (contains magnesium, do not use, check for lead), $CaOMgO$
- Tricalcium phosphate (very soluble)
- Dicalcium phosphate (very insoluble)
- Bone meal
- Calcium nitrate, $CaNO_3$
- Marl (check for magnesium, contaminants)

Figure 2

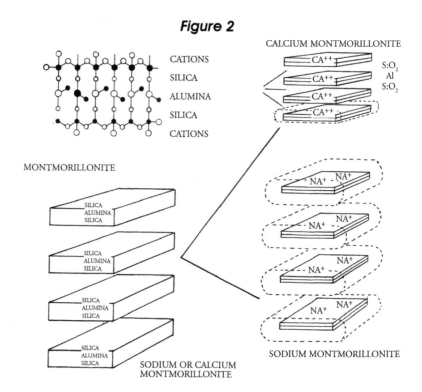

Figure 2 shows the structure of a typical clay particle. The comparison here is between calcium montmorillonite and sodium montmorillonite related to water absorption. The calcium will absorb only 1/4 as much water as the sodium. This is the problem with high-sodium soils: they hold a great deal of water, yet the crop starves for water. Carbon is the key to moisture in biologically active soil for it will readily store and give up water for plant usage. As more and more acid fertilizers are used and the calcium is depleted, greater amounts of sodium accumulate rendering the soil hard, salty, and sterile.

Calcium does some very interesting things in the soil. In the study of soil particle chemistry, you can observe the physical configuration of soil particles under various conditions. In compacted soils, there is usually a high concentration of sodium and/or magnesium ions. This creates a parallel plating action. When calcium is added, these particles flocculate, creating the basis for desirable soil structure. If extreme excess amounts of calcium are added, the particles will disperse, resulting in no structure. There is a balance in everything, but the point here is that calcium is a key element for desired soil structure and it is unrelated to pH. For further information concerning particle chemistry, it is suggested one start by studying petroleum engineering.

Figure 3

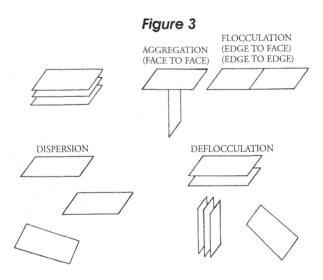

AGGREGATION (FACE TO FACE)

FLOCCULATION (EDGE TO FACE) (EDGE TO EDGE)

DISPERSION

DEFLOCCULATION

Figure 3 shows the various states of particle configurations. Aggregation is often the case in compacted soils. Flocculation is often the case in fertile, well-structured soils having adequate calcium biologically active. Deflocculation occurs when too much non-biologically active calcium is present. Dispersion is the result of excessive deflocculation and results in no soil structure at all. This can be caused by excessive amounts of elements other than calcium, but only if there is a deficiency of biologically active calcium.

The next element that needs to be addressed is phosphorus, usually referred to in its phosphate (P_2O_5) form. Phosphate is also currently neglected in fertilization programs. It is needed for proper nutrient transport and assimilation, but its most important function is that of energy transformation in photosynthesis to produce plant sugars. In the compounds ATP (adenosine triphoshate) and ADP (adenosine diphosphate), phosphate plays an important role in the breakdown and formation of metabolic compounds.

A good rule of thumb is that the higher the phosphate content, the higher the sugar content, and, correspondingly, the higher the mineral content. The sugars are the plant's energy storehouse. Also, the reduced nitrogen groups NH_2 and NH_3 combine with the carbon frameworks formed during the oxidation of sugars to form amino acids. In other words, if there is a phosphate deficiency there will be a sugar deficiency, and thus, an amino acid deficiency. Phosphate is an integral part of all metabolic processes.

Possibly the most critical process is the formation of nucleoproteins, the source of the genetic material. They are composed of proteins and nucleic acids. Nucleic acids are high-molecular-weight polymers of nucleotides, each formed from three constituents: a *sugar* (specifically ribose or deoxyubose), *phosphoric acid*, and a *nitrogen* base that has the structure of either a purine or a pyrimidine ring. Most people know nucleoproteins as DNA and RNA.

Phosphate is a relatively insoluble element, especially in the di- and tricalcium phosphate compounds. Here lies the irony. Many soils show a high level of phosphate, but in these insoluble forms. It requires rigorous biological activity to solubilize the calcium and phosphate, or strong reagent chemicals to break the bonding. Due to the nature of common phosphate fertilizers, 0-46-0 (triple super phosphate, which is highly acid), greater and greater amounts of soluble calciums and phosphates are becoming insoluble due to chemical reactions between the highly acid fertilizers and the soil compounds, and as a result insoluble compounds are formed. Most fertilizer specialists are either ignorant of this phenomenon, do not care, or deliberately ignore it, loading them to make recommendations which have resulted in widespread plant phosphate deficiency. Later, when food and crop quality is addressed, this will be covered in depth. The following is a list of phosphate sources:

- Soft rock (colloidal clay) phosphate (contains 26–33 percent calcium, 4 percent iron, and traces of many other nutrients) washings from phosphate ore) 14–28 percent P_2O_5 Hard rock phosphate (basically cleaned phosphate ore)
- Super phosphate 0-20-0 (rock phosphate reacted with sulfuric acid), 20.5 percent
- P_2O_5 triple-super-phosphate 0-46-0 (super phosphate reacted with phosphate acid — *avoid*)
- Dicalcium phosphate, diammonium phosphate (DAP) (granular 18-46-0 — *avoid*), also available in water-soluble crystal 12-52-0 (for special cases only)
- Monoammonium phosphate (MAP) (granular 11-52-0, water soluble crystal 12-62-0)
- Liquid phosphoric acid 78–85 percent, P_2O_5
- Bone meal
- Organophosphate (filtration byproduct, scrutinize closely)
- Ortho and poly liquid phosphates (be sure they are "clean," not industrial byproducts)

There are many sources in the marketplace. The selection and factors to consider will be addressed in Chapter 5, the program section of this book.

Potassium. This element is normally thought of in reference to potash (K_2O). Next to nitrogen, it is probably the most misused, overused, and abused element in agriculture. It is also the most profitable for the industry. Its basic function is to determine of the caliber or thickness of the stalk and leaves, fruit size, and number of fruit that sets. Used in excess, potassium will replace calcium in the cell structure, resulting in a diseased cell (i.e., one that resonates at a discordant frequency). A sure indicator of potash excess is the occurrence of black spots on the leaves. This is a typical occurrence in alfalfa today, and the farmer is told it is a disease or insect problem and should be sprayed for. Modern agriculture has become addicted to nitrogen and potash. Like any drug addiction, the requirement for the drug increases constantly. The farmers are told that in order to get more yield, add more nitrogen and potash. As the soil degenerates, it requires more of this drug to just sustain the crop yield. Potash does have its place in crop production, but it must be in balance with all other elements. The following is a list of potash sources:

- Potassium sulfate K_2SO_4, 45–52 percent, K_2O
- Potassium nitrate K_2NO_3, 13-0-46 46 percent, K_2O
- Chilean nitrate of potash, 15-0-14 14 percent, K_2O
  (*avoid* — high sodium content)
- Muriate of potash, KCL 0-0-60, usually 60 percent
- $9K_2O$ (most common source — *avoid like the plague!*)
- Sawdust wood ashes (use with caution — ashes
  dehydrate the soil)
- Tobacco stems
- Pecan hulls
- Cotton burr ash (use with caution)
- Straw rice hulls
- Sul-Po-Mag (check for chlorine; use only under
  prescribed conditions)

Nitrogen. Nitrogen, along with potash, is being overused, misused, and abused. It produces great profits for the fertilizer industry.

Nitrogen is the major electrolyte in the soil and living tissue. Without nitrogen there is no life. It is a primary component of protein and amino acids. Nitrogen is capable of entering the plant without phosphate, and given certain conditions it will carry potash with it. This condition, though typical of modern agriculture, creates a situation ripe for nitrate toxicity and nitrogen-funny protein formation (which occurs when there is a deficiency of phosphate and sugars), calcium substitution in the cell membrane, potash burning, and low sugar production from photosynthesis. This causes an overall mineral deficiency and, finally, the fallacy of current food production: plants that resonate at discordant frequencies, thus attracting rapacious insects; plants and soils infected with various diseases and stressed by environmental conditions; and plants that have poor nutritional value, short shelf life, and lack of flavor. (If there is a dead animal in the desert and one covers it with a canvas so the buzzards can't get to it, is the animal any less dead? Truly healthful food does not need man's omnipotent protection from insects and disease. It is inherent.) The air is about 78 percent nitrogen. Soil bacteria and plants have the capability of extracting much of their nitrogen needs from the air if they are allowed to do so.

Nitrogen is utilized by plants in two forms: nitrate NO and ammonia NH_4^+. Both have distinct functions. The nitrate nitrogen is needed early in the growing season to stimulate growth of leaf crops throughout the season. The ammonia nitrogen is needed later in the season for fruit and seed production. Don't expect tomatoes to set fruit if the nitrate nitrogen is high and the ammonia low. The two forms will readily switch back and forth from one form to the other depending upon the other nutrients in the soil. The following is a list of nitrogen sources:

AMMONIA NITROGEN SOURCES

- Ammonia sulfate, NH_4SO_4, 20.5 percent N (due to carbon content)
- Manures: cattle, bird, horse (be careful of hog manure due to high salt)
- Millorganite
- Sludge (scrutinize closely for contaminants)
- Tankage; dried blood
- Fish meal
- Urea
- UAN, 28 percent or 32 percent N (urea-ammonium-nitrate liquid blend)
- Household ammonia

- Anhydrous ammonia (avoid like the plague or convert to aqua ammonia)
- Aqua ammonia
- MAP — monoammonium phosphate
- DAP — diammonium phosphate
- Ammonium nitrate, provides both nitrogens

NITRATE NITROGEN SOURCES

- Sodium nitrate, $NaNO_3$
- Calcium nitrate, $Ca(NO_3)_2$
- Ammonium nitrate — provides both nitrogenous NH_4NO_3
- Chilean nitrate
- Potassium nitrate, KNO_3
- UAN, 28 percent or 30 percent, urea-ammonium-nitrate liquid blend

When purchasing nitrogen, know why it is being purchased. For example, usually you would *not* want ammonia nitrogen for lettuce. It may cause it to bolt and go to seed.

Carbon. Carbon is the element that makes anything organic. It is the primary buffer in the biological world. Without carbon there is no stabilization of nutrients. A carbon deficiency results in a carbon dioxide deficiency, which causes a carbohydrate and oxygen deficiency, harming the plant's primary functions. This in turn results in a decreased aerobic microbial life, reduction of the carbon cycle, and finally sterile soil. Carbon is a key element in the process of increasing the soil's magnetic field. When carbon is deficient, the nitrogens can form nitrogen-funny proteins, nitrites, and nitrous oxides, the latter two always toxic to biological life. Carbon is a key element for the formation of desirable soil structure, tilth, and water holding capacity. In the presence of excess boron relative to calcium, high salt, or sulfur conditions, a deficiency of carbon may allow ammonification to occur, which is fatal to aerobic life.

There are many forms of carbon. The form referred to as being vital to healthy soil is biologically active, that carbon that is vital to the living processes. A diamond is a carbon compound but not biologically active. Biologically active carbon is not always that found in humus. Under sterilization fertility programs the humus also becomes sterile and actually forms a carbon salt or chlorinate hydrocarbon. Notice that many muck farms that have been intensely farmed using classical methods. Observe when the sun shines on them how the soil looks gray-white rather than a shiny black. Also notice how dusty they are, how often they must be irrigated, and the soil is hard and compacted. Also notice the weed, insect, and disease war the farmers are fighting.

There are very few sources of carbon per se. It is an element best obtained by biological activity. Here are some good sources, depending upon your point of view:

- Manures
- Compost — excellent, generally speaking
- Leaves, sawdust, garbage, grass clippings — best to compost first
- Sugar
- Molasses
- Dry humates
- Liquid humic acid
- Peat — be careful! It is anaerobic
- Green manure crops (i.e., sweet clover, red clover, rye)
- Crop residue

You can apply tons and tons of carbon to the soil and still not obtain a good condition. The key to carbon fixation is aerobic bacteria. They do most of the work in the soil. These organisms are not pathological. They could possibly be compared to the baker who takes various ingredients and produces a desirable dish for us to eat. Aerobic bacteria such as *Sulfa ammonis*, *Nitrous ammonias*, and *Europa* put it all together in the soil. They convert elements and organics to usable forms. Without them all is for naught. Usually there is no need to add or apply these organisms to the soil, for if you simply provide a livable environment for them they will appear and proliferate on their own in good time.

The next several elements will be addressed only in passing, because once the foundation of calcium, phosphate, potash, nitrogen, and carbon are established the other elements can usually be supplied, if necessary, through fish and seaweed products. On occasion an individual supplement may be required.

Manganese. Manganese can be termed the element of life. It brings the electrical charge to the seed. It is the key element for seed and offspring production.

Iron. Iron draws energy to the leaf by absorbing heat. This makes the leaf darker.

Copper. Copper is the key to elasticity in a plant as well as mold control.

Boron. Boron is the key element for filling the center of stems and fruits. Hollow-stemmed grains and alfalfa and hollow heart or black heart in potatoes is an indication of a boron deficiency.

Chapter 3

The Agricultural
Industry

Adversity either brings more adversity or better conditions, depending on your point of view. Without adversity there would be no mechanics, no repair shops, no doctors or lawyers, no troubleshooters, no one pursuing better ways of doing things.

This section is intended to encourage the reader to evaluate his or her environment, see what he or she is really observing, and change one's conditions, situation, and environment for the better. If the food you consume is of higher quality than before, then you have changed something for the better. By the way, high-quality food does taste better. It is no wonder many people, especially children, do not care for many fruits and vegetables. There are very few nutrients and little flavor in those produced under most current commercial production practices. Children act by instinct. Their bodies crave sweets because under proper natural growing conditions the produce is naturally sweet, accompanied by all the minerals that should be there. Man defies this inherent natural quality by circumventing the correct fertility practices with nitrogen and potash. He follows this by adding extracted or synthesized salt and sugar to his food to fool the body's desire for minerals which would naturally accompany sugar. The result is a society of sugar addicts. To explore this further, let's investigate photosynthesis in a bit more detail.

Photosynthesis is the process whereby plants convert carbon dioxide and water into energy-rich organic compounds. All of

PHOTOSYNTHESIS
Light Phase
Photolysis (split H_2O molecule)

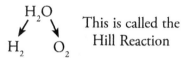

NADP accepts electrons & H_2 forming $NADPH_2$
Next, "light" energy is trapped in the process called
photophosphorylation ADP + "light" energy form ATP + PO_4
The next step is the "Dark Phase"

Dark Phase
$NADPH_2$ + ATP form the basic carbohydrate for energy

$$C_6H_{12}O_6$$

Initially there are 2 molecules of phosphoglyceric acid,
which finally give rise to a single, 6-carbon sugar and
eventually starch grains in chloroplasts.

NADP — nicotinamide adenine dinucleotide phosphate
ADP — adenosine diphosphate
ATP — adenosine triphosphate

the organic matter in living things is ultimately provided through photosynthesis.

The reverse of photosynthesis is respiration. The useful energy is channeled into chemical work, initially as high-energy phosphates. This energy is later used as needed in the production of organic materials for growth and development. Understanding photosynthesis and respiration will help in understanding three key principles: the importance of phosphate; phosphate's relationship to sugar; and the relationship of true quality (mineral content) to phosphate and sugar.

The irony of the system is that the plant scientist understands these principles (it is explained in detail in most science text books), but this understanding is not transferred to field application. Something happens to the information. Possibly the soil scientist misunderstands, though this is unlikely. Possibly there is a professional rivalry between plant and soil scientists that makes it feel deflating to acknowledge facts from research outside their specialty, or the information is not profitable for certain special interest groups.

PRACTICES AND PONDERANCES

It is said that practice makes perfect. Actually, perfect practice makes perfect.

First of all, let's cover soil testing. Soil testing can be a very valuable tool if interpreted properly. It can also be a catalyst for destruction.

First you need to gather the soil sample. If the area in question, whether it be ten square feet or eighty acres, is going to be fertilized with the same materials at the same rate, then it is unnecessary to submit more than one composite sample for testing unless you are curious about specific areas. Gather the sample from the top four inches of the soil. Take several samples from around the area in question and mix these samples together. Take about one cup of this mixture as the composite, put it in a soil sample bag or some container that will maintain the soil's integrity. Label the sample as area number such-and-such, or garden or field. List the plants to be grown and previously grown, your name and address, and the type of test requested. In addition, it is recommended that your personal records include the date and type of volunteer vegetation (weeds, etc.) growing, earthworm abundance, etc., data that can be referred to later to check progress. I will cover three types of analyses. All three have their value. Again, interpretation is the key.

The first test is typically referred to as a general state or CEC test. It is done by the land grant universities via the cooperative extension service, or any number of private laboratories. These labs use acids stronger than those naturally present in the soil to extract the nutrients from the soil sample. The quantities of each nutrient are recorded on a computer printout, and if recommendations have been requested they will be given according to the recommender's arbitrary interpretation system.

The greatest value of these tests is that they give a ballpark estimate of what nutrient quantities are potentially available for plant growth. Since the extraction chemicals are stronger than those used by the plants, to assume the test results correspond to the availability of plant nutrient is erroneous. Plants cannot go to the nearest lab and get strong extraction solutions. The test helps you determine what you have to work with as a foundation. Sometimes these nutrients can be made available to the plant by triggering chemical reactions with fertilizers, but the best way is to establish rigorous microorganism activity that produces biological compounds easily assimilated by plants. An analogy could be made to a miner who calculates the output of his mine as if he were digging with a case of dynamite when all he really owns is a pick and shovel. The arbitrary recommendations from this kind of test are of little value to the progressive agriculturalist.

An article in the February 1983 issue of *New Farm* magazine described an investigation of soil test recommendations from 70 prominent soil test laboratories all over the county, including several state university and private labs. Not one test result on one fertilizer recommendation was consistent with another. The labs were, however, consistent in one area. They recommended an average of $41.98 per acres of unneeded fertilizer. In all fairness to these labs, the writers of the article had their own arbitrary recommendation system, and it had the same void as the labs it criticized: no consideration for crop quality (mineral content) or the chemical and biological repercussions of the fertilizer materials used. A 2013 study performed by the University of Kentucky revealed that large differences in recommended amounts and types of fertilizer had virtually no impact on yields. High fertilizer usage and costs did not lead to higher yields.[1] The best advice is simply to take the soil test report for what it shows (nutrient quantity using certain extraction solutions) and discard the recommendations.

The following is a copy of a typical soil test report from Michigan State University.

SOIL TEST REPORT

The pH of 5.5 indicates the soil is on the acid side. As well as being a measure of acidity and alkalinity, pH is also a measure of

---

[1]This study is available online at http://www2.ca.uky.edu/agc/pubs/agr/agr1/agr1.pdf.

resistance. The higher the pH, the greater the resistance and vice versa. Nutrients in all biological life, including soil, are transported via electricity. The resistance to that transport is important, yet pH is only a measurement of the result of the nutrient ratios in the soil. The pH is not something to worry about changing. It changes as the nutrient ratios change, therefore, if you work at restoring proper nutrient balance in the soil, the pH will take care of itself.

Most university and private labs suggest an ideal soil pH of 6.5 to 6.8. For the purposes of this discussion, work on restoring the soil fertility and not being concerned with good or bad pH values.

The suggested pounds per acres for the various nutrients varies by lab and by crop. For this test and crop the suggested values for phosphorus, potassium, calcium, and magnesium are: phosphorus at one hundred pounds; four hundred pounds; not applicable because pH only is considered; and seventy-five pounds per acre, respectively.

The cation exchange capacity (CEC) value of 8 corresponds to the soil texture of 3. The sandier a soil, generally the lower the CEC. The greater the clay content, the higher the CEC and the higher the humus content of any soil texture, the higher the CEC. The CEC indicates how much nutrient the soil can store.

The percentages of total exchangeable bases for potassium, calcium, and magnesium are 14.5, 82.6, and 2.8, respectively. These can be correlated to the pounds per acre figures mentioned previously for deriving a ballpark idea of what kind of soil potential you have to work with. Generally speaking, looking at this type of soil test we would like to see calcium above 80 percent exchangeable base and greater than 2,000 pounds per acre; magnesium at least less than 20 percent exchangeable base with no real pounds per acre figure; potassium between 10 and 20 percent exchangeable base and a pounds-per-acre ratio of one pound potash to two pounds phosphate. Please keep in mind that this type of test is closer to a mining survey as far as its relationship to what is biologically active and available for plant growth is concerned. This type of test is used extensively in agriculture today by universities and many private labs to recommend fertilizer programs, but that doesn't automatically mean those programs are what should be used. The state of our soils and foodstuffs points up this fallacy.

Figure 4

MICHIGAN STATE UNIVERSITY, EAST LANSING, MICHIGAN 48824
SOIL TESTING LABORATORY

BRUCE ANDERSEN
2499 CANNONSVILLE NW STANTON48888
MONTCALM

TEST RESULTS	
SAMPLE NO	1
SOIL PH	5.5
LIME INDEX	65
LBS. PER ACRE OF:	
PHOSPHORUS	268
POTASSIUM	183
CALCIUM	533
MAGNESIUM	11
PARTS PER MILLION OF:	
ZINC	
MANGANESE	
COPPER	8
CALC CEC	
PCT. ORG MAT	
PCT. OF TOTAL EXCHANGEABLE BASES:	
POTASSIUM	14.5
CALCIUM	82.6
MAGNESIUM	2.8

****

IF MANURE IS USED CREDIT 4# N, 2# P205, AND 8# K20 PER TON APPLIED

RECOMMENDATIONS

****

SAMPLE   1

PREVIOUS CROP: WHEAT

FUTURE CROPS:		EXP. YIELD	NIT. N	PHOS. P205	POTASH K20	B	ZN	MN	CU	NOTES
				---LBS PER ACRE---						
1ST YR	OATS + LEGUME	50-79	25	0	75	-	-	-	-	1 *
2ND YR	ALFALFA-TOPDRESS	5-6	0	200	2.0	-	-	-	-	
3RD YR	ALFALFA-TOPDRESS	5-6	0	200	2.0	-	-	-	-	

LIME NEEDED FOR PH 6.5= 4.3 T/A.
LIME NEEDED FOR PH 6.8= 4.7 T/A.

1 MAGNESIUM TESTS LOW. USE DOLOMITE AND/OR A SOLUBLE MG SOURCE.

* MAXIMUM RECOMMENDATION FOR ACP COST SHARING   0 LBS P205/A.   150 LBS K20/A

Alfalfa will pay at this on/off? time now and feed mtopdsing/or, agridertilthis orumek.

****

SAMPLE DATA		
ACRES	10	LAB 19503
SOIL TEXTURE	3	PAID
MANURE	0	TRAY 045
PLOWING DEPTH	9	FOR FURTHER RECOMMENDATIONS SEE YOUR C___'TY AGENT

28   *The Anatomy of Life & Energy in Agriculture*

Next, we look at the recommendations. The previous crop was wheat, and future stated crops are to be oats seeded over a legume (alfalfa). Recommendations are given for three years, an arbitrary figure. The expected yield for oats is 50 to 79 bushels per acre with a recommended fertilizer application of 25 pounds of nitrogen and 75 pounds of potash per acre. For the second and third year, the expected yield is five to six tons per acre of alfalfa with a recommended fertilizer application of 200 pounds of potash per acre and two pounds of boron per acre. Next, the recommended lime application is 4.3 tons per acre to achieve a soil pH of 6.5 and 4.7 tons per acre to achieve a soil pH of 6.8. The special note mentions a magnesium deficiency; therefore, dolomite lime or a soluble magnesium source is recommended. Next, under the government's cost-sharing program for fertilization, it will pay for no phosphate fertilizer and will share the cost for 50 pounds of potash. Finally, the local extension agent in his written comments states that alfalfa won't grow at the soil pH of 5.5 and recommends liming first and seeding (planting) later.

The unfortunate thing about this report and its recommendations is the damage this information inflects on the soil and plants. To begin with, the first recommendation calls for combining oats and a legume (alfalfa), yet the extension agent states alfalfa won't survive under this soil condition. If a crop cannot survive, on what is the test recommendation based? Next it recommends top dressing the second and third year alfalfa with 200 pounds per acre of potash and two pounds of boron. As a feed, alfalfa is a calcium supplier, yet potash is the nutrient perpetually recommended. Alfalfa is a legume, which means it has rhizobium nodules on its roots for fixing nitrogen (taking nitrogen from the environment and supplying it to the plant). Since there is a phosphate deficiency in this fertilizer program, there will be an imbalance caused by an excess of nitrogen. In the presence of excessive nitrogen, the unneeded potash will enter the plant as potassium nitrate. This creates a potash imbalance which makes it possible and probable that it will replace the already low amount of calcium — low due to the phosphate deficiency. The result is a weakened plant cell that resonates at a discordant frequency attractive to insects. In addition, the potassium nitrate creates a watery cell that shrinks greatly at harvest and causes nitrate toxicity in the consumer. The excess potash also produces black spots on the leaves due to its burnings, which the "experts" label, among other things, as bacterial leaf spot or common leaf spot so the farmer can purchase a pesticide to combat the *symptom* rather than correct the cause, which is the excess potash he was advised to purchase originally.

This is very easily verified. Take a refractometer, an instrument used to measure the carbonhydrate content of liquids (further discussed in Chapter 6), and check the sugar reading of the alfalfa. If the reading is below 12 or 14, there is a serious phosphate deficiency which allows for a potash excess. The real proof can be found by checking the growing number of alfalfa plantings where the farmers have ignored the "experts" and fertilized the alfalfa with calcium and phosphate. The refractometer readings are as high as 28–30. There are no black leaf spots, no insect pests, no hollow stems, no nitrate problems, no mold problems, and there are yields in excess of ten tons, and they are profitable farmers.

The next recommendation is for liming based upon pH. The type of lime suggested is dolomite. First, pH is not a measurement of quantity or volume, and certainly is not a measurement of calcium. (Check with any competent chemist.) Three tons of the highest-calcium lime were applied to this field during the previous fall, yet the test doesn't show any sign of it. So much for the test. The key is in making this calcium *available* to the plants. As for dolomite lime, it generally runs from 15 to 35 percent magnesium. Now, the recommended level of magnesium, according to the MSA extension service, is about 75 pounds per acre. Therefore, you need to add 64 pounds to achieve the recommended level. If you apply the lesser recommended amount of 4.3 tons of lime per acre, you'll apply 4.3 tons x 2,000 pounds per ton x 15-45 percent magnesium carbonate = 1,290 pounds to 3,870 pounds of magnesium carbonate, or 374 pounds to 1,122 pounds of elemental magnesium. This is five to fifteen times the needed recommended amount. It costs the farmer extra money because dolomite lime is more expensive than high-calcium lime and it creates a tremendous imbalance of nutrients. Many people think if a little is good, a lot must be great. That's true for love, but not fertilizer. High-calcium lime, which generally runs between

2 and 5 percent magnesium, would provide adequate magnesium for this field.

Then there is the cost-sharing program. The government will share the cost of one thing, potash. There is nothing like perpetuating a bad thing. Of course it's only bad for the soil. Consequently it is bad for the alfalfa grown on it, the consumers of the alfalfa, the farmer who is paying for this manipulation, and you, the consumer who pays in the end. It is great for the fertilizer and chemical company and the university that receives research money to perpetuate this vicious cycle. If the author sounds a bit perturbed about this circus, I am. The proof is in the results. The field in question, on which the soil test was done, was planted at the end of April 1985, with alfalfa and oats. The soil was sprayed before planting with a fertilizer solution formulated from scratch using an electronic scanner. One week after planting, prior to seed sprout, there was a severe wind storm. A neighboring field was eroded so severely by the wind that one could not see across the field, yet the field in question did not suffer even though it was bare. The oats grew wonderfully and were harvested green for cattle feed, and the alfalfa, which grew to 18 inches in height before winter, covered the field uniformly. The fertilizer mix was as follows:

	1985 PRICE	2013 PRICE
4 ounces humic acid	$0.31	$0.78
8 ounces bacteria water	.625	2.00
6 pounds potassium carbonate	3.00	3.00
5 pounds calcium nitrate	.38	1.70
3 pounds corn sugar	.78	1.80
1 ounce seaweed	.25	1.00
5 pounds monoammonium phosphate	3.50	5.00
1 ounces ascorbic acid	.50	1.00
	$9.35	$16.28

All of it was mixed and applied in a solution of 25 gallons of water per acre. (Only two of these products are recognized as fertilizers by the experts, calcium nitrate and monoammonium phosphate.) The real difference is that this farmer truly cares about his soil, his animals, and the public who finally consumes his product.

Included here is the 1986 soil test report from Michigan State University for the same field. The pH has jumped from 5.5 to 7.1, yet no lime was added since the first test. Also, the magnesium has been added. The recommendations are consistent in principle — little or no phosphate and lots of potash — yet inconsistent in quantity per ton of alfalfa. As usual, no consideration for quality is mentioned. The main points about soil testing and the resulting recommendations are: the testings are of little or no value in and of themselves, or relevant to quality plant feeding, because it is strictly laboratory oriented and unconcerned with the living aspect of soil fertility and plant growth. The recommendations are based on predetermined standards irrelevant to anything except fertilizer and chemical sales. The quality aspect — meaning the Brix, which reflects the mineral content of the crop being grown — is never considered.

The fertilizer prescription which was formulated using an electronic scanner and applied to this alfalfa field on May 10, used the following per acre:

8 ounces humic blend	1 ½ quarts calcium solution
12 ounces Clintose corn sugar	25 gallons water per acre

We often hear of people who slaughter the English language. But what about the people who slaughter basic chemistry and physics, and ultimately our soils? There is no argument; modern agricultural practices have cost us half our topsoil and given us toxic chemical nightmares. No soil — no food. No food — no life.

A more worthwhile soil testing practice is being done by a few private labs and many individuals. This system utilizes the Le Motte testing equipment according to procedures developed by Dr. Carey Reams and Dr. Dan Skow. It uses an extracting solution closer in strength to what plants possess. It also checks both the ammonia and nitrate nitrogens. Recommendations are generally consistent because they consider crop quality and fertilizer quality as part of the program. This test gives the client a better starting point from which to begin improving the living states of the soil in question. Unfortunately, as in all wet chemical testing, there is still an arbitrary interpretation of test results based on man-made parameters.

Figure 5

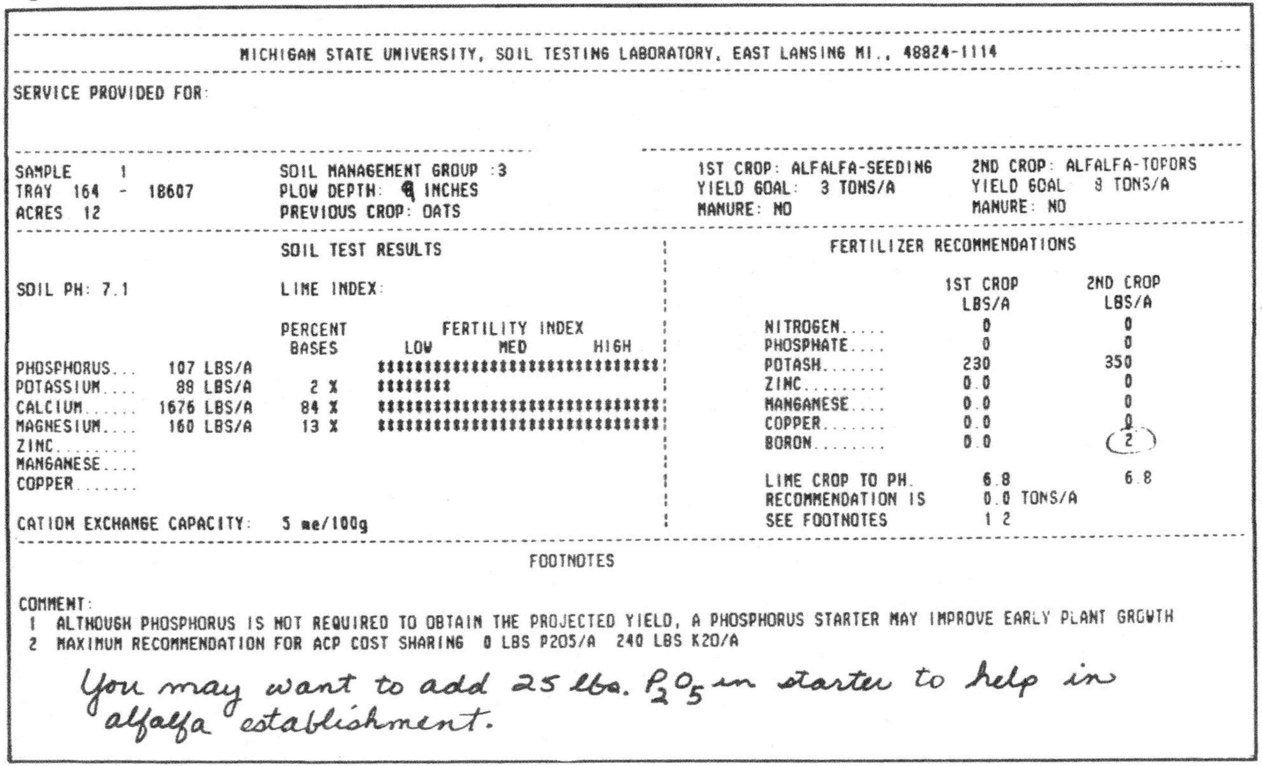

MICHIGAN STATE UNIVERSITY, SOIL TESTING LABORATORY, EAST LANSING MI., 48824-1114

SERVICE PROVIDED FOR:

SAMPLE 1	SOIL MANAGEMENT GROUP :3
TRAY 164 - 18607	PLOW DEPTH: 9 INCHES
ACRES 12	PREVIOUS CROP: OATS

1ST CROP: ALFALFA-SEEDING
YIELD GOAL: 3 TONS/A
MANURE: NO

2ND CROP: ALFALFA-TOPDRS
YIELD GOAL: 3 TONS/A
MANURE: NO

SOIL TEST RESULTS

SOIL PH: 7.1

LIME INDEX:

	PERCENT	FERTILITY INDEX		
	BASES	LOW	MED	HIGH
PHOSPHORUS	107 LBS/A	##############################
POTASSIUM	88 LBS/A	########
CALCIUM	2 %	1676 LBS/A	##############################
MAGNESIUM	84 %	160 LBS/A	##############################
ZINC	13 %		
MANGANESE		
COPPER		

CATION EXCHANGE CAPACITY: 5 me/100g

FERTILIZER RECOMMENDATIONS

	1ST CROP	2ND CROP
	LBS/A	LBS/A
NITROGEN	0	0
PHOSPHATE	0	0
POTASH	230	350
ZINC	0.0	0
MANGANESE	0.0	0
COPPER	0.0	2
BORON	0.0	0

LIME CROP TO PH.
RECOMMENDATION IS 0.0 TONS/A
SEE FOOTNOTES 1 2

6.8
6 8

FOOTNOTES

COMMENT:
1 ALTHOUGH PHOSPHORUS IS NOT REQUIRED TO OBTAIN THE PROJECTED YIELD, A PHOSPHORUS STARTER MAY IMPROVE EARLY PLANT GROWTH
2 MAXIMUM RECOMMENDATION FOR ACP COST SHARING 0 LBS P2O5/A 240 LBS K2O/A

You may want to add 25 lbs. P₂O₅ in starter to help in alfalfa establishment.

Here are the suggested values for nutrient levels using the Le Motte system for a healthy soil, in pounds per acre:

Calcium (Ca)	2000+
Phosphate (P_2O_5)	400
Potash (K_2O)	200
Sulfate (SO_4)	200
Nitrate nitrogen (NO_3)	200
Ammonia nitrogen (NH^+)	40
Iron (Fe)	40

This system, usually referred to as the Biological Theory of Ionization, is a grand step ahead of conventional theories. People who understand this system have obtained marvelous results to prove its validity. There are also many failures attributed to the program, but upon investigation every one was the result of hastiness, incomplete understanding of the program, incomplete application of the program, or the use of inferior or contaminated products, unbeknownst to the purchaser.

This brings us to the third method of testing. Like the second over the first, it is a step up. This method involves the use of an electronic scanner. The particular one used here is a type of spectrometer that measures biological and non-biological energies of the phi field, the electrostatic scaler potential. (For those readers who would like more technical information, I suggest investigating advanced level physics courses as well as reading the work of Thomas E. Beardon, available from his website: cheniere.org.) The net result of this testing program is that available fertilizer products can be checked with the soil for their electrical compatibility before they are applied. The skilled technician or consultant can put together a soil fertility program based upon the soil's actual response to the fertilizer product. Those readers familiar with applied kinesiology can understand the process. It is an advance beyond the arbitrary, cook book, trial and error, I hope it works, we did it last year, copycat system that has lost this country one-half of its topsoil in the past 100 years, depleted the quality of its food, and polluted its environment — all in the guise of progress. Remember, plants and soils do not read books. One hundred years ago doctors were appalled at the suggestion of washing their hands between patients to prevent the transfer of little organisms one could not see (without a microscope) called bacteria. Because the doctors did not believe these organisms existed did not change the fact they did. Today you would be appalled if the doctor did not wash between patients.

There are two other practices related to testing that warrant a mention. Both are performed conventionally and have elicited a great deal of printed material. One is the CEC test in conventional soil test systems. A numerical value is calculated from the lab for the given soil sample. This figure is then used along with the soil pH to determine the theoretical amount of lime necessary to change the pH to a predetermined figure. It looks very nice on paper and sounds very sophisticated (and it is), but not in agriculture. The cation exchange capacity is a value relating to capacity of, particularly clay, particles to hold cations, i.e. Ca^{++}, Mg^{++}, Na^+, K^+, NH^+, etc.

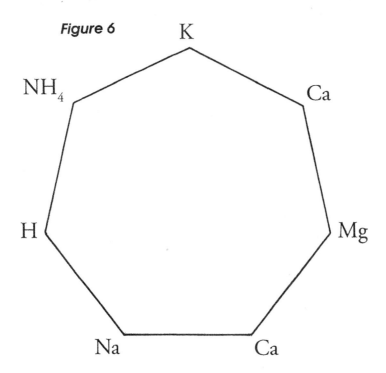

Figure 6

K

NH_4

Ca

H

Mg

Na

Ca

This analysis was developed by the mining industry and is mainly used by petroleum engineers for formulating drilling muds that will carry the debris away from the drilling bit. It is basically a raw chemical/physical phenomena and is out of context when used in a biologically active soil and a progressive fertility program. Possibly it is a contributing factor in the mining of our soils.

The CEC, though used extensively, is of very little value in agriculture. The test was adopted by the agricultural industry as a tool to perpetuate the manipulative fertilization practices of modern agriculture that have led to the mining of the soil.

Also worth mentioning is the tissue test. Tissue analysis is the laboratory analysis of fresh plant vegetation. It is widely used. There are some very successful consultants and agriculturists who perform tissue analysis. It is done regularly throughout the growing season in an attempt to find nutrient deficiencies in the crop, followed by a foliar feed to correct it. It is correct in theory and it can work in practice. There are, however, two pitfalls. One, it often takes several days to several weeks for a report to return on the testing. By this time the plant's growth stage has changed and something else is also a problem now.

The other pitfall has to do with standards. Who decides what the nutrient levels should be? Most often these levels come from research analysis of healthy plants. Who decides what is healthy? If the crop required any chemical sprays to protect it from insects or diseases, it was not healthy! Since most publicized research is done by scientists who do not recognize the validity of the last statement, the values given as standards for tissue analysis only allow the farmer to produce more of the same and then buy a rescue chemical. Looks can be deceiving, especially if you do not see what you're looking at. Again, the two pitfalls of tissue analysis can be rectified with the use of an electronic scanner; the crop can be analyzed in the field immediately and a recommendation presented that will correct any deficiencies that are feasible to fix.

Time is of the essence. Problems are developing and growing at accelerated rates. It takes nature between 30 and 100 years to replenish just one inch of soil. It is currently being lost at about five to eight times this rate. Why are the soils fading at all? Experts suggest it is due to increased production intensity, careless tillage practices, and improper ground cover. Though that sounds convincing, it is only toying with symptoms. It does take the monkey off the culprit's back, or seems to. The culprit is improper soil and plant nutrition. Conventional fertility practices have reduced the magnetic properties of the soil to the point where it cannot hold itself together. Try making some cookies without any flour. Once the magnetism of the soil is reduced then the elements — wind, rain, and snow — can easily remove the soil. Following are some major culprits of magnetic degradation.

Muriate of potash. Often called red potash, white potash, kalium potash, 0-0-60, and 0-0-62, muriate of potash is potassium chloride (KCl). It is the most commonly used potash fertilizer in this country. Ironically, its chlorine content makes it one of the most detrimental products that can be applied to the soil. Muriate of potash contains an average of 40 percent chlorine. When this product comes in contact with acids or acidified fertilizers such as 0-46-0 (triple super phosphate — the most commonly used commercial phosphate fertilizer), the chlorine will form muriatic acid (commonly known as hydrochloric acid), which will destroy any bacteria it contacts and will acidify the soil, causing such minerals as calcium and iron to become less available in the soil solution should they contact the muriatic acid.

The chlorine that does not become muriatic acid combines with calcium, magnesium, and especially sodium to form chloride salts that are also detrimental in the soil, as they cause dehydration, adverse pH changes, and salinization. When potassium chloride contacts nitrate nitrogen (NO_3) half the chlorine forms hypochlorous acid (HClO), the main chemical used as a swimming pool disinfectant. This compound is very hostile to bacteria, and thus inhibits their growth. The other half of the chloride forms chlorine gas which sifts into the air. Chlorine gas is also toxic to biological life, including people. It is a gas *heavier* than air, therefore it lies close to the surface of the land and in low areas. When chlorine gas contacts water from high humidity or rainfall, some of it forms more hypochlorous acid and may fall as acid rain. The remainder recycles as chlorine gas. Unfortunately, potassium chloride is like a drug to the soil — the soil gets hooked on it. As with any drug addiction, increased amounts are required yearly to achieve the same "high," eventually causing the death of the user. The use of potassium chloride also leads to more compacted soil — due to the destruction of organics it causes — requiring more power for tillage, more chemicals for pest control. This chain reaction, begun by the destruction of the organics, leads to increased erosion.

Furthermore, the use of potassium chloride for fertilization leads to eventual desertification from salinization and then, most important of all, it leads to the production of poor quality — mineral deficient — crops. There are many alternatives to potassium chloride — potassium sulfate, potassium nitrate, potassium hydroxide, Chilean nitrate of potash, and several organic sources, including potassium carbonate, all of which do not contain chloride. It is imperative to purchase only products that do not contain chloride.

Ironically, farmers are told that potassium chloride is not detrimental to the soil, even though professional chemists and petroleum engineers insist that chloride is extremely harmful to the soil. The bottom line is that potassium chloride causes the demise of soil fertility, leading to the need for more and more fertilizer, greater amounts of pesticides and larger and more powerful equipment. It is time for the farmer to become aware of the peril he is creating, take his own interests in hand and turn the situation around. Only the farmer himself is truly concerned with his own interests.

It is argued that chlorine does not hurt anything because there is such a small amount of it actually applied, and "research" proves it. Anyone who is familiar with research and statistics knows that the parameters of a research project determine its universality. It is important to find out what those parameters are. How much chlorine does it take to do harm to a biological system? Municipal water supplies are normally chlorinated to kill bacteria, good or bad. The concentration of chlorine is between one and two parts per million. At 10,000 drops per pound, eight pounds per gallon, that is one drop of chlorine in 12.5 gallons of water. If you have a swimming pool, you are familiar with chlorinating it to keep the organisms in check. Note that a pH test is included in swimming pool test kits. As the chlorine content increases, so does the pH.

That says something for the value of using pH as a calcium (lime) indicator, especially if you consider how much chlorine is applied via fertilization.

Let's calculate just how small the amount of chlorine applied to the soil really is. Muriate of potash, KCl, contains about 40 percent chlorine or 40 pounds per 100 pounds of KCl. A one-acre slice of soil 43,560 square feet by six inches deep is generally said to weigh more or less 2,000,000 pounds. If a farmer applies 100 pounds of potassium chloride, he has applied 40 pounds of chlorine. To calculate the chlorine concentration, assuming the fertilizer is a dispersed evenly throughout the six inch slice of soil, you would take 40 pounds of chlorine divided by 2,000,000 pounds of soil and get 20 parts per million of chlorine, or about ten times that needed to kill the microorganisms. The truth is that most farmers apply several times that amount, some as much as 1,000 pounds per acre, of potassium chloride each and every year. Chemistry is chemistry whether it is in your swimming pool, the public water supply, or the soil. It is the aerobic microorganisms in the soil, alive and active, that make the soil fertile. Chlorinate the soil and you inevitably suppress them.

The use of muriate of potash or potassium chloride is not the only degenerative practice commonly observed. Almost as detrimental is the use of industrial wastes. These include spent acids such as phosphoric or sulfuric acid that are first used by industry and then used to make fertilizers such as ammonium sulfate, liquid sulfur, liquid monoammonium phosphate and various other liquid blends. Not all fertilizer companies do this, but many do. These raw materials are cheaper than clean product because industry has already used it once. From their industrial use these products pick up any number of heavy metals like lead, cadmium, or aluminum. When these cheaper fertilizers are applied to the soil, the heavy metals cause problems with the microorganisms and in many cases, contrary to cover-up reports, are taken into the crop, thus causing problems for the consumer. The intake of whole molecules by plants is a principal of science no longer under dispute.

Another possible problem product from industrial waste is by-product lime from processing plants, paper or pulp mills. This type of lime can be loaded with metals, but is more often full of resins or toxic chemical complexes. These chemicals can be extremely bad for the soil, yet they are widely used because the soil scientist says it will do such and such for the pH. He does not even consider checking its nutrient value or potential hazards.

The next practice involves the misuses of a potentially valuable product — anhydrous ammonia. This is one of the most popular and widely used forms of agricultural nitrogens. It is a very profitable product for its manufacturers. "Anhydrous" means the water is removed, leaving only ammonia. The product is fine if water is added to get what is referred to as aqua-ammonia. Anhydrous ammonia is extremely dangerous. It can severely burn the skin. It can also burn the lungs and rapidly suffocate a person by displacing oxygen. It is very effective in destroying organics — so good, in fact, that in 1942 the U.S. Army used it to make emergency air strips. When a farmer applies anhydrous, he uses a tool that knifes the ammonia several inches into the soil. It effectively reduces the usable oxygen in the soil needed by the aerobic microorganisms, burns the organics that include the microorganisms, creates an ash, and sets in motion the process by which formaldehyde and pathological organisms abound. Case in point: Dr. Dan Skow remembers when he first started his veterinary practice in the early '70s, anhydrous ammonia use was as scarce in his area as chlamydia in hogs. As anhydrous ammonia usage became more and more popular, so did chlamydia in hogs on those same farms. Today it is a serious problem requiring regular vaccination on the farms that use anhydrous ammonia. Anhydrous is a cheap source of nitrogen, though. It looks good monetarily in some programs on paper, but, again, chemistry is chemistry. Another common practice of "modern" agriculture that degrades soil fertility is the use of dolomite limestone.

Dolomite lime. Dolomite lime is a compound of calcium carbonite and magnesium carbonate. It ranges in magnesium content from 15 percent to 35 percent. It is commonly used as a liming material when institutional soil tests indicate a soil magnesium deficiency. Magnesium is often overused in present-day agriculture. There are many publications that profess magnesium deficiency, substantiated by the fact that the symptoms disappear after magnesium application. Unfortunately this is the same logic used to justify all the accepted fertilization and pest control practices that have resulted in the fiasco of modern agriculture. The main problem with dolomitic lime is that it contains too much magnesium. According to Michigan State University's soil tests, the recommended amount of magnesium per acre for fertile soil is in the range of 75 pounds. Using the pH logic for liming, they recommend using dolomite if there is a magnesium deficiency because dolomite will raise the pH and provide the needed magnesium as well. Let's assume your soil has zero pounds of magnesium by their test and pH logic recommends applying two tons of dolomite lime per acre. Using the value 25 percent magnesium as the lime's average magnesium content, you would be applying 2,000 pounds x two x 25% = 1,000 pounds of magnesium. By MSU's standard, the soil needed about 75 pounds of magnesium, or about 1/13 of that present in two tons of dolomite lime with 25 percent magnesium. Dolomite lime is 20 percent to 30 percent more expensive than high-calcium lime, and the excessive magnesium creates a severe mineral imbalance in the soil. If you ask why the extreme excess is recommended, you will be told it is for reserve purposes. Fact: reserves are only useful and beneficial if they are in proportion with all other components. Any element in excess causes a toxicity. Selenium is a very important trace element, but apply 13 times the needed amount and the result will be fatal.

Magnesium carbonate will readily form magnesium nitrate salt ($Mg\{NO_3\}2 - 6H_2O$), which is strongly hydroscopic (has an affinity to water). The chemical reaction here has a dehydrating effect. This reaction can also produce a nitrogen deficiency that requires the farmer to purchase more nitrogen. Also, this compound increases the salt content of the soil, increasing the potential for root and crop dehydration (burning), and finally increasing the possibility of both magnesium and nitrogen being leached out of the soil (magnesium nitrate is very water soluble). The so-called reserve is wasted and/or deleterious. Adequate magnesium is present as an impurity of high-calcium lime, and most soils already contain adequate magnesium despite claims to the contrary.

An additional drawback of dolomite limestone is that it is often contaminated with lead. There is no nutrient value in lead. It is toxic. It adds additional stress to an already overstressed, undernourished soil. Before you swallow the argument that lead is found in such small quantities that it doesn't hurt anything, think about how much it takes to hurt the current U.S. fertility situation, and remember the adage "the straw that broke the camel's back."

There are several other agricultural practices that seem to look good, especially to someone with tunnel vision. One of these practices is what can best be termed the single-nutrient fix. There are many publications with beautiful photographs of various plants with various nutrient deficiency symptoms. Ponder for a moment. Nature is much more complex than this. Deficiency symptoms are the result of a chain reaction of events that the current system does not take into account. If you have a rust spot on your car that has come through from underneath, does it correct the rust problem to say there is a paint deficiency and paint over the spot? People who live in areas where large amounts of road salt are used realize that the paint can often mask a growing rust problem but does not correct it. Here lies the major flaw in the single-nutrient fix philosophy. Quality. When that nutrient is added to the crop, did the health and quality (mineral content) improve as well, or has the real problem been masked? Remember the rule: nutrients must be accompanied by phosphate to be properly assimilated by the plant. If there is a phosphate deficiency, there is a deficiency of all other nutrients.

Nitrogen can get in and can carry potash with it, but this is not good because it results in less than optimum cell structure, watery plants, nitrogen toxicities and insect infestations.

The following four examples of the single-nutrient fix philosophy are the ones commonly promoted by soil scientists.

The proclaimed deficiencies were taken from miscellaneous publication 47 of the Fertilizer Institute, Washington, D.C., *Be Your Own Corn Doctor,* by K. C. Berger.

A *phosphate shortage* makes reddish-purple marks on leaves, particularly on young plants. It is actually a copper and manganese deficiency that causes the plant leaves to turn these colors. The reason there appears to be a phosphate deficiency is due to the fact that all nutrients must be assimilated in phosphate form. Technically there is a phosphate shortage, when the phosphate is considered the carrier or escort of the copper and manganese. A deficiency of these two elements actually causes the visual symptoms.

Potash deficiency appears as a firing or drying along the tips and edges of lowest leaves. Here there is actually a carbohydrate and molybdenum deficiency. Since carbohydrates are products of photosynthesis and phosphate is the key element in photosynthesis, the carbohydrate deficiency can be technically attributed to a phosphate deficiency. As this is the case, then the molybdenum also does not have adequate phosphate to escort it. The reason potash appears to eliminate the symptom is that it is applied as muriate of potash (KCl), which will convert to potassium nitrate and then which move into the plant. Potassium nitrate readily carries a great deal of water containing carbon dioxide with it. This carbon dioxide temporarily supplies enough carbon to partially correct the symptom. The potassium chloride also creates a localized pH change in which more molybdenum is available, because the limited amount of phosphate will grab onto that which has the least resistance to movement in the solution. The pH here is the measurement of that resistance, thus a little more correction of the symptom. The nitrate nitrogen carried in with the potash corrects the rest of the symptom.

Hunger sign is yellowing that starts at tip and moves along middle of leaf. This is actually a carbohydrate and boron deficiency under circumstances similar to the alleged potash deficiency. The nitrogen is carried in water, which contains some carbon dioxide, and the nitrogen creates a localized pH change in which boron is more available for the phosphate to latch onto.

Magnesium deficiency causes whitish strips along the veins and often a purplish color on the underside of the lower leaves. This symptom is, loosely speaking, a magnesium deficiency. Technically, there is a nitrogen toxicity here, and magnesium is the antidote for pulling out the nitrogen by forming magnesium nitrate that is then flushed out of the plant, making the symptoms disappear. Symptoms may disappear after a single-nutrient fix, yet the cause behind them usually remains. Test: if the refractometer reading increases, you are on the right track. (Refer to Chapter Six for further discussion on refractometers.)

NORMAL EAR, BIG EAR, SMALL EAR

Normal ear on well-fertilized, high-producing corn weighs about 2/3 of a pound. It has well-filled tips.

Big ears weighing up to one pound indicate that the plant population was too small for most profitable yields.

Small ears are usually a sign of low fertility. For better yields, boost fertilizer application.

These axioms all based upon opinion and suboptimal standards. The question that needs to be asked is, "Normal, big, or small ear compared to what?" First of all, the size of the ear is directly proportional to the nutrition available during its development. Take two ears of equal size and weight them. The heaviest one has the greatest mineral content. Commodities are measured by weight not volume, so if you have a 60-pound test weight corn, there will be less volume versus a 56-pound test weight corn.

When you base your observations on mineral content using a refractometer to evaluate crops, you will know that none of the ears pictured in this bulletin are very good compared to what they should be for feed or food. There is too much denting of the kernels. Not one of them would have a refractometer reading of 12 or above. Another factor regarding these first three ear descriptions is that you could possibly find all three on the same stalk.

EAR DEFICIENCY SYMPTOMS

Phosphate shortages interfere with pollination and kernel fill. The ears are often small, twisted, and have undeveloped kernels.

Potash shortage shows up in ears with poorly filled tips and loose, chaffy kernels.

Nitrogen is essential throughout the growing season. If a plant runs out of nitrogen at a critical time, the ears will be small and have a low protein content. The kernels do not fill at the tip.

The true deficiencies are the same as those discussed for the plants.

Green silks at maturity may be caused by too much nitrogen in relation to other elements. Green silks are actually caused by deficiencies of calcium, phosphate, and manganese.

Regardless of what the soil test values are, or what some textbook may state as necessary level of phosphate, if there is a low level of sugar, then there is a deficiency of assimilated phosphate and other mineral nutrients. There may be something blocking the phosphate assimilation or an actual phosphate deficiency, but it is none the less a phosphate deficiency. Until it is corrected, no true picture of the other nutrient deficiencies is possible.

There are many factors that can contribute to a nutrient deficiency. The blocking of a nutrient creates a deficiency of that nutrient. This is quite common. Remember, all nutrient phenomena are related to electromagnetism. If there is too little current flow, the system is sluggish and some of the nutrients, especially the heavier atomic weight elements, will not move at all. If there is too much current flow, the system is hyper and burning often occurs or, so to speak, electrocution occurs. Picture a train on a schedule that is coordinated with other trains using the track. If the train is too slow, stoppages occur. If the train is too fast, there may be collisions or derailments. Too little current flow in the soil is caused by too much alkalinity, often attributed to areas of high limerock concentrations. This is fairly easy to correct, especially using an electronic scanner for product selection. Too much current flow in the soil is not quite as quickly corrected because it is often caused by salt buildup in the soil; it can also be caused by too much acidity. High salt buildup also occurs in alkaline soils, a compound problem common to U.S. soils. Salt buildup has two major causes: the destruction of organics by toxic fertilizers and the use of high-salt fertilizers, both of which destroy organics.

The use of materials such as muriate of potash and triple super phosphate add salt to the soil. The salt dehydrates the soil, causes excess current flow, and therefore creates more salt by burning the soil. It also causes excess current flow, thus creating still more salt by burning out still more organics. As the organics are depleted, the soil becomes compacted and biologically inactive. The organics hold the magnetism that holds the soil together. This cycle perpetuates itself, especially with the annual addition of salt fertilizer. Also, when large amounts of chlorine are applied to the soil, the organics disappear, and increasing amounts of soil nutrients form chloride salts that dehydrate the plant and are easily leached out of the root zone. More and more water is required to the point where eventually the soil can become saturated with water, even though the crop is starved for water. The next step is desert.

The bottom line concerning all these practices is that they directly or indirectly destroy the organics — biologically active carbons — that determine the soil's vitality and fertility. Just because the farmer applies manure or tills in large amounts of organic matter (crop fodder, residue, or cover crops) does not guarantee it will be converted to humus. Organic matter can take two pathways: anaerobic, resulting in organic salts, formaldehydes, and soil demise, or aerobic, resulting in humus soil maintenance and rejuvenation. Once either cycle is in motion, it takes a tremendous countermeasure to change it. The present-day phenomena of erosion, nutrient leaching, environmental pollution, massive applications of chemicals to rescue the crops, storage problems of produce, nutrient deficiencies in consumers, and most of the horrendous costs of production are all symptoms of misuse and abuse of the soil. It is not unique to this decade, as Dr. Charles Northern pointed out back in the 1920s. The situation has just intensified to the point where more people are starting to take notice and ask questions.

The counter response to the discussion in this chapter is similar to that of a person cursing a lifeboat destined to save him from a sinking ship, as if it showed weakness or insult toward the victim to be saved. It sometimes portrays the saying "Don't confuse me with the facts, I've already made up my mind." How sad. So many people see only the immediate profit of this self-destruction, which is a very short-sighted view because even the "recognized" scientists agree that if it is not reversed, there will not be a future in which to spend those illustrious profits.

Why do farmers get response and growth from some of the practices and products addressed previously? Remember that plants and all biological life lives and grows from energy. Anytime two substances react, energy is exchanged. There is no question the application of muriate of potash (KCl), dolomite lime, waste acids, salt fertilizers, anhydrous ammonia, and single-nutrient fixes produce chemical reactions, which net some energy that causes plant growth and often changes the visual appearance of the crop. But there is more to it than what meets the eye. Putting ether in a diesel engine will produce a response, but it's not a preferred practice. You can use airplane fuel in an automobile, but how long will the engine last? Unfortunately, we are not dealing with an engine here. We are dealing with the very sustenance that keeps this planet and its inhabitants alive. We are not playing games with politics, computer games, sporting events, or the stock market. We are dealing with our lives, our children's lives, and so on. One must consider more than the short-term visual observation. If you truly see what you are looking at, you will observe that such phenomena as the crop turning dark green after an application of nitrogen is only a nitrogen green and not synonymous with a quality green.

Farmers have often been heard saying they aren't concerned with quality, just volume, because they are selling the crop anyway. What would you think of a doctor or pharmaceutical company with that attitude? If the facts are truly understood, you can get more volume from high-quality crops than low quality, and much more economically. In response to the concern that U.S. farmers already produce too much, some light will be shed on that propaganda at the end of this book. What truly is a quality crop? What characteristics does it exemplify over what is currently, boastfully proclaimed as good quality crops?

Chapter 4

Divine Blueprint

Nature, the environment in which we live, is not haphazard and not without order and purpose. From the smallest single-celled organism to man, there is a purpose and a place for everything, and everything has its place and purpose. As you gain an understanding and appreciation of life, you will discover that there is no need for man's intervention. Only when man disrupts this balance and then proceeds to circumvent and overrule natural laws does there appear to be chaos and brutality in nature. Nature will triumph in the end whether man cooperates in harmony with it or plunders away into oblivion. Man does have the capability to help nature regenerate, however. This is a marvelous wonder to observe. Nature will more than take care of man if he simply allows her to do so. She will also protect man if left to her own devices.

There is a simple experiment that can be performed to show that electromagnetism is a key principle of nature. Take a sample of some fertile soil, preferably from a wild forest, flower patch, or some other area relatively free from human interference, and then take a sample of poor, infertile soil. Put each in a separate glass test tube and suspend each one by a thread so they hang freely. Then take a 2,000-gauss cobalt magnet and move it close to each tube. The more fertile soil is paramagnetic and will be attracted to the magnet, and the less fertile, diamagnetic sample will be repelled. Use beach sand as the poor fertility sample to get the most distinct reaction. Since the more fertile a soil, the greater its paramagnetism, it only stands to reason that there is correspondingly less erosion.

There are distinct indicators in nature corresponding to the level of fertility — health and vitality — of the soil. Let's start with insects. Most people are taught to believe that insects are just pests, and as such are just there to be pests. Insects have a very distinct and important task: they devour. Each species of insect has in its genetic structure a specific food for it to devour, and that food is determined by frequency. Dr. Philip Callahan of the University of Florida, a USDA entomologist, explains that insect antennae are actually like small semiconductors and, as they are coated with wax, are also paramagnetic structures. They receive various wavelengths in the infrared spectrum. Once the information is received, the insect's brain determines whether the frequencies correspond to a mate, food, water, or something else. Everything emits infrared radiation, and each thing has its own specific range of vibration. The vibrational frequency of all the component parts of a thing makes up its composite vibrational frequency. This is what the insect receives and processes.

If a plant is in perfect or near-perfect health (mineral balance), it will vibrate at a given composite frequency. If there happens to be a mineral deficiency, it will vibrate at a slightly different composite frequency. If there is a serious deficiency or several deficiencies that make that plant unfit for animal or human consumption, it will vibrate at a significantly different frequency that the insects know as food, hence an insect infestation. This phenomenon is easily proven. Grow a plant, a potato for instance, according to the program that is laid out in the next chapter of this book, and also grow one according to conventional practices. Keep track of the sugar (Brix) readings and notice which plant is devoured by insects and which is not. Once the quality of a crop surpasses a given level, there will not be an insect problem with it, because the crop will not vibrate at a composite frequency corresponding to the insect's food.

Diseases are self-destruct or red-light mechanisms with the same purpose — to signal a mineral deficiency or imbalance. Correct the deficiency and the disease disappears. You can prove this for yourself by the same method as for the insects, only this time monitor the potato plant for blight or some other malady. When you grow a vegetable of higher quality, notice the flavor, texture, color, shape, size, weight, density, storage life, aroma, and energy derived from eating it. High-quality produce will not rot. It will only dehydrate.

The next so-called pest is the weed. Weeds seem to be everywhere in the lawn, the garden, the flower box, alongside the road, in corn fields, and in hay fields. It is often said that fertile soil will grow weeds and crops equally well. That is only if you are growing weeds as a crop. Like insects and diseases, weeds have a distinct purpose — to replenish the soil. It may take nature decades or centuries to correct man's fiascos if left alone, but nevertheless it eventually will. Weeds are the best soil test you can use. Each weed species is genetically keyed to replace a specific deficiency. For simplicity's sake, they are divided into three categories: broadleafs, grasses, and succulents. Generally speaking, broadleaf weeds are present to correct the imbalanced ratio between phosphate and potash. The ratio should be two parts phosphate to one part potash for row crops and vegetables and four parts phosphate to one part potash for grasses. These values are based upon the use of the Le Motte testing equipment following the Biological Theory of Ionization procedures. Typically, you will find the ratios not only reversed but as bad as ten parts potash to one part phosphate. Also, the broadleaf weeds act to detoxify chemicals in the soil through metabolic processes.

Grasses such as foxtail and quackgrass are generally present to correct a calcium deficiency. In permanent crop areas such as orchards, grasses can be effectively used as a fertilizer simply by keeping them mowed and allowing the clippings to compost back into the soil. In areas where the clippings will not compost back into the soil but rather create a thatch buildup, there is a lack of aerobic microorganisms, an excessive salt concentration and poor aeration.

Succulents are usually present to replenish the carbonate ions in the soil as well as increase its water holding capacity. Succulents also act as a ground cover to protect the fragile soil from erosion and dehydration.

As you garden or farm, keep records and truly observe things, you will notice the unfolding of some very interesting events. The use of fertilizer will determine what types of plants will be healthiest. If you fertilize for weeds, then weeds will be the healthiest plants growing. The laws of nature do not change simply because man writes a book of theories contrary to natural law. The electronic scanner has made it possible to perform some inexpensive evaluations which can then be verified by observation, Brix readings, and wet chemical laboratory analysis. The following is a brief example, compliments of a good friend, of three different plants' responses to various fertilizer materials. Two are considered major weeds — buttonweed (or velvet leaf) and foxtail — while the third is Golden Glow corn.

BUTTONWEED (VELVET LEAF)	VITALITY
Weed in field	660
Muriate of potash (KCl)	850
Magnesium sulfate ($MgSO_4$)	850
Potassium sulfate (K_2SO_4)	650
Bladex herbicide	540
Molasses	500
Cobalt sulfate ($CoSO_4$)	300
Phosphoric acid	200
Vinegar	180
Soft rock phospate	150
2,4-D	120
Lignite	110
Manganese sulfate ($MnSO_4$)	110
Lime (source A)	40
Molybdenum	0
Composted chicken manure	0
White corn sugar (Clintose A)	0

FOXTAIL	VITALITY
Weed in field	350
Muriate of potash (KCl)	600
Zinc sulfate ($ZnSO_4$)	500
Potassium sulfate (K_2SO_4)	290
Copper sulfate ($CuSO_4$)	250
Lignite	200
Manganese sulfate ($MnSO_4$)	190

Soft rock phosphate	130
Lime (source A)	60
Phosphoric acid	80
White corn sugar (Clintose A)	0

GOLDEN GLOW CORN	VITALITY
Corn in field	1400
White corn sugar (Clintose A)	5200
Manganesee sulfate ($MnSO_4$)	5100
Soft rock phosphate	4700
Molasses	3300
Lime (source A)	2600
Lignite	2100
Lime (source B)	1000
Zinc sulfate ($ZnSO_4$)	800

The way to interpret this data is first observe the weed or corn-in-field vitality. This is the scanner value for that plant, as it exists in the field. Next, as the various fertilizers are put with the weed or corn, the vitality of the weed or corn changes. For example, applying muriate of potash to velvet leaf raises its vitality to 850, meaning it is a very good, beneficial fertilizer for velvet leaf and will increase its growth. Note that the good weed fertilizers are the poor corn fertilizers. Remember, quality mineral balance is the standard. The function of every weed is to replenish the imbalance of minerals. Therefore, the greater the imbalance, the better the weed grows. As the imbalances are corrected or deficient nutrients replaced by proper fertilization, the weed is no longer needed and its growth and vitality fade.

Check manganese sulfate on all three plants. It reduces the weed's vitality and increases the corn's. Notice that lime (source A) and soft rock phosphate are poor weed growers and good corn growers. Take special notice of the effect the organics — molasses, lignite, clintose A corn sugar, vinegar, and composted chicken manure — have on the corn versus the weeds. The organics provide the energy and carbon for the microorganisms to proliferate as well as for the corn to grow healthfully. None of these organics, except the manure, are recognized or registerable as fertilizers, yet muriate of potash, which is detrimental to corn and any fertile soil, is not only recognized and registerable as a fertilizer, but also portrayed as the best source of potash for the farmer to buy.

Another case worth mentioning is that of zinc. Zinc has become a highly recommended trace element by the experts and institutions. The response that follows the addition of this element is illusory. Zinc applications generally enhance weed growth and may cause a deceptive visual change in the desired crop, but zinc applications per se do not improve the quality of the crop. The supposed zinc deficiency symptoms are actually nitrogen deficiency caused by a phosphate deficiency. Nitrogen is an electrolyte and so is zinc. Therefore, its application "corrects" symptoms but not the cause behind the cause. There are cases in very depleted soils such as those found in Western Australia where zinc is truly deficient and needs to be added.

When walking through a garden or field, notice which plants seem the healthiest. Which ones are being devoured by insects and diseases, the weeds or the crop? As crop quality improves, the Brix content will increase, the mineral content will increase, and the storage life will lengthen. Correspondingly, these values for the weeds in the same area will decrease. If you wish to investigate the effect fertilizers have on weeds in greater detail, observe plant and insect occurrences, keep notes, and experiment with your own plants. A further listing and explanation of the previous type of plant and fertilizer comparison can be found in the book *When Weeds Talk* by Jay McCaman, available at Acres U.S.A.

Once the balances of nature are restored or at least closely approximated, your soil will improve yearly with fewer and fewer inputs per output required. This is easily calculated. Remember the rule of thumb: 80 percent comes from the air, 20 percent comes from the soil. This concept is a very important, especially when coupled with the fact that there is as much plant mass below the ground as there is above. Putting the two together, the picture looks as follows: If you are growing a corn plant and harvesting the entire plant, how is the soil gaining? Let's say we remove one hundred pounds of dry matter in corn plants. Eighty percent, or eighty pounds, came from the air and 20 percent, or twenty pounds, came from the soil, so the soil is minus twenty pounds of nutrients. Since there is an equal amount of mass below the ground (the root system), then there is also a hundred pounds there. Twenty percent or twenty pounds came from the soil, and 80 percent or eighty pounds came from the air. Since the plant material below ground is not removed by harvest, the soil receives a new gain of one hundred pounds minus another twenty pounds, which was required from the soil to make up the underground portion. That twenty pounds remains, but is not a net gain, so the net gain to the soil is sixty pounds, or 60 percent of the quantity that was harvested. This is sixty pounds of organic material, including carbohydrates, enzymes, vitamins, and minerals, to add to the soil's fertility *provided* there is a living biological system to process it. If not, it becomes a salt or formaldehyde that will perpetuate degeneration of the soil. Nature will continue to exist and prevail either way. Man can either fight her and curse her to his demise, or he can peacefully co-exist with her to his health and wellbeing, following the divine blueprint.

Most of the products that are good for the corn and bad for the weeds are not recognized by the experts, and in most states are not even registerable as fertilizers. So much for the consumer protection by state agencies and institutions.

We actually have two hundred pounds of dry matter of which only one hundred pounds are removed from above the ground.

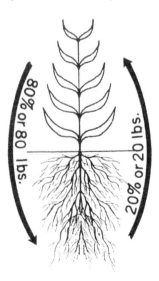

For every hundred pounds of dry matter removed above the ground, there will be a net gain over the above the one hundred pounds of sixty pounds of dry matter added to the soil, provided the biological system is in order. This is true farming, being a caretaker of the earth. Present-day agriculture is actually mining, as proved by the continued demise of our soils.

Remove one hundred pounds dry matter, there is equal dry matter above the ground as below. Eighty percent of one hundred pounds comes from the air. Twenty percent of one hundred pounds comes from the soil. Therefore, we have actually removed twenty pounds from the soil.

We have added eighty pounds below ground from the air. We have removed twenty pounds from the soil by removing one hundred pounds above ground, therefore, we have a net *gain* below ground, in the soil, of sixty pounds dry matter, provided the system is functioning properly.

Chapter 5

The Garden

At last we are at the beginning. Gardening, whether in a single clay pot or on a window sill or on 15,000 acres, is meant to be a joy, something you appreciate and take pleasure in doing. It is also a very important and serious undertaking. Anytime a person grows a plant for human consumption, directly or indirectly, they have taken the responsibility for the outcome of that undertaking. It is often said that the computer age is making life impersonal and indifferent. Growing food does the opposite. It is a very personal activity. Do not grow food because it is a fad, because some health book demands it, or because a friend or spouse wants you to. Don't do it for any reason other than you choose to voluntarily and lovingly. Don't do it grudgingly because good quality food is difficult to find in a store. Do it joyously. Enjoy it genuinely and the rewards will come accordingly.

There are several new start-up groups present in 2014 that were not around in 1989 when Acres U.S.A printed the first edition of this book. There is HighBrixGardens.com, Remineralize.org, and RealFoodCampaign.org, among others. The Real Food Campaign group, which is now called the Bionutrient Food Association and was a brain child of mine from a number years ago, wrote out a plan for consumers to get on the website, learn about the refractometer, evaluate the foods they purchased, and record them. This data would then go into a central database, which would be shared with members of the website. I gave this information and design to Dan Kittredge who then started the Real Food Campaign website that is helping to educate consumers about Brix and food quality from a nutrient perspective.

A small company started by John Kempf in Ohio, Advancing Eco-Agriculture (GrowBetterFood.com), is one of the leading bio-fertilizer companies to date, integrating Steiner's, Schauberger's, Reams's, and Albrecht's teachings into products for both organic and biological farmers. Other excellent garden and farm manu-facturing companies include Lancaster Ag Products (LancasterAg. com), FHR (FHR1.com), MicroLife Organic Fertilizers from San Jacinto Environmental Supplies in Houston, Texas (SanJacSuppply. com), and Tainio Technology (Tainio.com). There are a number of companies in Australia, New Zealand, and South Africa that are ex-cellent biological farming support companies. A central contact in New Zealand would be Phyllis Tichinin at TrueHealth.co.nz and in Australia David von Pein at TheMeterman.com.au. In the Nether-lands there is NovaCropControl.nl. Nova Crop Control is the next generation of nutrient testing, having developed a proprietary sap extraction and testing methodology and nutrient value parameters that actually correlated to plant health, disease, and insect infesta-tion. It is much better than standard plant tissue testing. These all can be found on the web. Further, I recommend the gardener look at ARBICO-organics.com for natural pest control, as they grow beneficial insects.

Soil. The better the soil is prepared at the beginning, the faster and easier your progress will be. First, the materials to be applied must be applied to the surface and tilled into the top two to three inches only. Apply the following in order to start the building pro-gram:

PER ACRE	PER 1,000 SQ. FT.	PER SQ. FT.
Soft rock phosphate, 200–500 lbs.	12 lbs.	1/5 oz.
High-calcium lime, 1,000–2,000 lbs.	23–46 lbs.	3/8–3/4 oz.
Ammonium sulfate, 100 lbs.	2.3 lbs.	4/10 oz.
Compost, 500–2000 lbs.	12–184 lbs.	2/16–3 oz.

If compost is unavailable, any good organic such as liquid or dry humates will work fine. Raw organics such as leaves, manure, and grass clippings should be either composted first or applied in the fall so they can be digested by the soil. If they are applied in the spring, the energy required to digest them in the soil will be robbed from the growing crops thus stunting their growth. Soft rock phosphate, high-calcium lime, and compost are the base ingredients necessary to begin establishing a stable, fertile soil. Please keep in mind that there are many ways to accomplish the same goal. It is good policy to walk before you run.

Once these products are applied, till them into the top two to three inches of soil, preferably using a roto-tiller about three to four times in several different directions. However, do not attempt to substitute an alternate phosphate for the soft rock phosphate. If you are going to use the building program, use the products suggested. Substitutions and alternatives will be covered later. Also, in regard to ammonium sulfate, the one recommended is dark, grayish-black material from Allied Chemical Company or a feed fermentation plant. This product is unique due to the carbon it picks up during the industrial process. This unique characteristic greatly helps regulate the temperature of the soil by keeping it warmer during cool periods and cooler during hot periods. As long as there is some calcium available in the soil, there is an interaction here.

For those who are worried about the use of commercial fertilizers, you have every right to be concerned. There are many detrimental commercial products on the market; likewise, there are some equally detrimental "natural" products such as potassium chloride, calcium chloride, wood ashes, dolomite lime, and certain manures and composts. It is similar to the human supplement industry, where regardless of the claim for purity and "naturalness," some products are excellent, some are poor, and some are atrocious. Fertilizers are no different. Use the available products, commercial or not, that will increase the productive capacity and quality of the soil and crops as rapidly and without compromise as possible. Use the refractometer to verify changes in plant quality. (Refer to Chapter 6 for further explanation of refractometers.)

Once the tilling is complete, let the soil sit idle for two weeks. If it is powder dry, water once or twice during those two weeks. Till the soil once more to prepare the seed bed and begin planting. This may seem like excessive tilling, but remember we are building the soil, and therefore we need microorganism life. These organisms need oxygen to live and proliferate. Proper roto-tilling aerates the soil as well as mixes the nutrients evenly. To set up the best magnetic field for growth, you need a well-dispersed nutrient base, not one in strips or with pockets and clumps. Thorough mixing of the nutrients into the soil is paramount.

Alternatives and substitutions. If you are just not able to obtain the products listed because of unavailability or financial distress, don't despair. There are alternatives and even a "no budget" program. If there is a will, there is a way. Collect all the eggshells, chicken, turkey, and other animal bones available. Take a hammer and crush them as finely as you can. Lay newspaper down to save the fine powder; it is most valuable. Then collect all the food scraps, meat scraps, grass clippings, leaves, and weeds you can find. Compost everything together. Work this compost into the top two to three inches of the soil at a rate of one ton (2,000 pounds) per acre, 46 pounds per 1,000 square feet, or one ounce per square foot minimum. You can hardly apply too much of this compost. If you have no soil, simply make some. Find some broken cement blocks or bricks (do not use asphalt). Crush them with a hammer as finely as possible. Mix one part compost and one part crushed cement. The result is excellent soil at no cash expense.

There are some good pre-mixed materials on the market that combine several materials in addition to the ones mentioned above. Accordingly, you should expect to pay for the convenience of pre-measurement and mixing. Be alert to ingredients that contain chlorine, such as potassium chloride. Many products say "all natural" and still contain this ingredient. Check the sources of the ingredients. Be sure there is no misunderstanding about what is being purchased. If there is doubt about chlorine content for example, either ask for a sample for analysis or a written guarantee that the product is chlorine free.

During the growing season additional fertilizer may be desired. One very good source is the weeds growing in the area. Incorporate them back into the soil or compost them. Remember, as the soil improves, there will be fewer and fewer "weeds." There are two ways that midseason plant foods can be applied, either foliar fed through the leaves or applied to the soil in liquid or dry form. On truck or commercial farms where large areas are planted to the same crop, there is little thought given to fertilizer interference. In small gardens or plantings, however, it is of major concern.

Interference can happen when you fertilize a fruit or seed-producing vegetable so it will set fruit, that is, tomatoes, pepper, peas, beans, melons, squash, eggplant, corn, cucumbers, etc., when there is a leafy or non-fruit vegetable close by or next to it, such as celery, lettuce, broccoli, cauliflower, radish, carrot, romaine, endive, onion, collards, or cabbage. What may happen is that the leafy vegetable will bolt and go to seed as well. The reverse can also happen. If you fertilize a leafy vegetable to encourage more growth, the possibility exists for the fruit producer to drop its fruit or blossoms or not set fruit. It is therefore recommended that leafy and fruit-producing vegetables not be intermixed within a garden where fertilizer interference may occur. Gardeners often have beautiful lush vegetation but very little or no vegetables at harvest. This doesn't have to happen. It has nothing to do with the seed or variety. If the products mentioned earlier are applied during the previous fall or early in the spring, there should be little need for additional fertilizer during the growing season for most vegetables.

If you need to improve the vegetable quality even more, then foliar feeding (feeding nutrients through the leaves) is by far the best way to go about it. Successful foliar feeding, like any other successful fertilization, should not be done randomly. It is best done during the quarter before full moon, worst done during the quarter before new moon. First, there must be adequate calcium in the soil, and if there is not, it has nothing to do with pH. Foliar feeding will not remedy a major calcium deficiency. Calcium is the foundation upon which the rest of the plant is built and needs to be in the soil. Some relief can be had by foliar feeding.

You might as well try building a house without a foundation or frame. Secondly, you must have a good fertilizer product, meaning no industrial waste acids, no chlorine, and no chemicals or heavy metals. Starting with the least sophisticated method, you can use a shotgun approach to foliar feeding by simply spraying a diluted solution of hydrolyzed fish or seaweed or both. Follow the label directions for mixing. Mix in a small misting bottle and lightly mist the desired plants. It is not necessary to soak or wash the plants with this spray; a light mist will suffice. This kind of spray is generally beneficial to all vegetable and crop plants, some more than others and some areas or times more than others. It is important to monitor the results with a refractometer.

The next, more sophisticated step, is to pre-test various solutions on a single plant using a refractometer to determine what product or combination of products are best at that given moment. This allows for more specialization and quality improvement. Check the Brix value of a plant in the row or field in question using the refractometer. Next, lightly mist the plant or area with a spray solution. Wait 30 to 45 minutes and recheck with the refractometer. If the value is less than or equal to the original value before spraying, then do not spray the remainder of the plants or field at this time. If the refractometer values have increased, then the spray is beneficial. If one has several different sprays, use the one that raises the refractometer value the greatest. These may and probably will change from day to day or week to week. Always keep records so patterns can be observed.

The most sophisticated method currently practiced is the use of an electronic scanner, covered in Chapter 9, to formulate a specific prescription from scratch for the plant(s) in question. This allows for maximum efficiency and quality improvement. One very important rule to remember is that the symptoms of a specific nutrient deficiency, such as manganese, copper, or potash, may or may not mean that specific nutrient is deficient. The symptoms often indicate a phosphate or complementary nutrient deficiency. Usually fish or seaweed products provide sufficient trace nutrients. Once the foundation nutrients of calcium, phosphate, carbon, potash, and nitrogen are balanced, then the others will usually be in balance. There are exceptions to the rule. If the addition of a trace element raises the Brix value of the plant in question, then it was needed.

Fall fertilization should follow the same guidelines recommended at the beginning of this section. Roto-till five to six inches deep or plow first. Apply soft rock phosphate, high-calcium lime, compost, and ammonium sulfate. Roto-till two to three inches deep two to three times for thorough mixing, and finally spread some type of cover crop for the winter, such as oats, rye grass, wheat grass, red clover, etc. When spring arrives, you will only need to roto-till a few times to incorporate the cover crop and plant. It is also recommended that you repeat the fall program for several years. Compost and cover crops should be applied indefinitely. The application of fertilizer materials should be regulated by the quality status of the crop growing. As the crop improves in quality and you use scraps from the crop for compositing, then the quality of the compost will also improve accordingly, thereby reducing the need for supplemental fertilizer.

Composting. This process is the key to all the life cycles on this planet. It is the process that enables elements and nutrients to be recycled for use by growing plants. Composting gives nutrients to the biologically active organic forms essential to self-sustaining soil. As a rule of thumb, every pound of carbon in compost has the capacity to hold four pounds of water. Composting is the natural process of converting organic matter to humus. It is a simple, worthwhile operation. Just gather all the organic scraps available from leaves, grass clippings, and table scraps to animal manures, if available. Then some agricultural lime (calcium carbonate or calcium oxide, not calcium hydroxide, which is also called hydrated lime because it is too caustic) or bone meal and soft rock (colloidal clay) phosphate. Mix about three pounds of lime and two pounds of soft rock phosphate to each 100 pounds or organic material. Thoroughly mix and turn the compost pile once a week. For best results, keep the rain and sunlight off the compost. The compost must reach approximately 144 degrees Fahrenheit; add some water to cool it. There will usually be no problem with excess heat if you avoid horse and hog manure. By incorporating the lime and soft rock phosphate into the compost, those materials will be much more available for plant growth when applied and you won't need to add them to the compost mix. If the temperature of the compost pile gets too high, then the organic material will turn to ash, and in extreme situations it will look like wood ashes. If you purchase compost, be alert to this and check to make sure the organic matter is completely composted. If it is not, then you will be able to identify the organic material as grass, leaves, or whatever. Once the compost is complete, you can add 50 percent sand and to make an excellent potting soil. Or you can purchase good potting soil and then add the lime and soft rock phosphate to it. If you do this, do not start seeds for at least two weeks. If you choose to be a little more sophisticated with the potting soil, then the following recipes may be appropriate:

Recipe 1
10 pounds composted cow pen manure
10 pounds sphagnum peat moss
80 pounds garden soil
8 pounds calcium carbonate
4 pounds soft rock phosphate
2 pounds sawdust

Recipe 2
10 pounds compost
30 pounds sphagnum peat moss
60 pounds white sand
8 pounds calcium carbonate
4 pounds soft rock phosphate
2 pounds sawdust

Recipe 3
70 pounds white sand
25 pounds sphagnum peat moss
5 pounds chicken manure
8 pounds calcium carbonate
4 pounds soft rock phosphate

Let these mixes set for two weeks before planting seeds. The reaction of the soft rock phosphate with the soil is energy intensive and excessive for seed sprouting. If you are planting young plant sets, there will be no problem.

Before planting seeds, put the seeds in a glass of distilled water. The best, most highly mineralized seeds will sink to the bottom of the glass while the poorer ones will float. Do not use the floaters. However, if they are the only seeds you can obtain, then use them. Next, purchase some Seed Soak and soak all seeds for two and half hours. Plant according to the specific recommendations from the seed company. Keep the potting soil moist, and water once or twice a week with Nutri-Feed or another product that does not contain chlorine. This product may also be used as a foliar for the young plants. Some crops you might consider starting early from seed are cucumbers, watermelon, tomatoes, green peppers, celery, cauliflower, and broccoli.

When you transplant these plant sets to the garden or field, put one-half teaspoon of soft rock phosphate in the bottom of the hole, along with some water. And if you are transplanting fruit trees, berry plants, or shade trees, dipping the roots in a mixture of mycorrhiza; fungi, inoculant, or compost tea is ideal. Another dip for dipping roots is:

100-Ounce Batch
85 ounces water w/ inoculant or compost tea
2 ounces humic blend
8 ounces calcium solution
2.5 milligrams iron sulfate
5 ounces corn sugar (dry)
5 milligrams copper sulfate (dry)

Mix all components in order. Iron sulfate is a liquid and is best used as the product Ferro-Tonic. Mix the two dry materials (corn sugar and copper sulfate) and then add as one.

Also be sure that the side of the stem or stump with the most roots is planted facing north. This will prevent many plant deaths. Lastly, add several drops of the homeopathic solution Rescue Remedy to every dipping solution for the shock of transplanting.

Plant layout. Though there is no carved-in-stone right way and wrong way for laying out a garden or truck farm, there are some general guidelines and practices that can help assure success. Avoid interplanting fruit-producing vegetables with leaf or foliage-producing vegetables, avoid interplanting watermelon and cantaloupe due to cross pollination, and avoid planting tomatoes next to zucchini squash — the squash will get sick and die. Never plant gourds in or near the garden because they can cross pollinate and taint the flavor of edible vegetables.

To make the maximum use of space, install a wire fence and firmly anchor it. Beside it plant tomatoes, beans, and cucumbers. Train these plants to grow — prune the lower branches or any growing below eight to ten inches above the ground as well as about one quarter of the intermediate branches. This enables the plant to produce larger fruit right up to frost time due to less competition. Remember, a lush growth of foliage does not automatically mean there will be a bumper harvest of fruit. Often the opposite is true. It is also advisable to place the crops according to maturation time, squash next to corn, pickles next to peas, etc. Match the maturity dates.

Again, there are no really definite right and wrong practices. Each person will prefer a slightly different plant layout. The goal is healthy produce and personal enjoyment. Have fun at it.

There are a few helpful hints to keep in mind while growing food. Avoid applying chicken manure compost on strawberries because it will make them taste woody from the high boron content of that particular waste product. Apply 100 to 200 pounds per acre, two and one half to five pounds per 1,000 square feet, one-twentieth to one-tenth ounce per square foot of Sul-Po-Mag between July 15 and September 15 to the garden, especially orchards and trees, to increase sap flow.

Avoid all chlorinated products and water. If you must use city water, then apply it through a fine mist sprinkler. This will help evaporate some of the chlorine that will then hopefully be blown away by the wind. One may have a fungus problem even in the city water for chlorine will not eradicate fungus. Purchase a small hose injector unit and inject four ounces per 100 gallons water of 3 percent household hydrogen peroxide into the water. This practice will curb fungus and many disease contaminations that are fungal in nature. Avoid using wood ashes. They are high in potash, and most soils have already had excess potash applied due to typical fertility recommendations. Ash will dehydrate the soil and further interfere with the soil's improvement.

Generally do not till or cultivate tree crops or orchard plantings. This injures the roots and creates tremendous stress on the trees and vines. Plant grass and mow, mow, mow.

One more helpful hint: diatomaceous earth is an effective product with which to dust pets for the control of fleas, ticks, and lice, as well as for dusting plants and plant beds to control many insects. Diatomaceous earth is a non-toxic and beneficial material.

An interesting potato-growing project is to take a large wooden barrel, remove one end, and put a hole in the other for water movement. Put a two-inch layer of sand on the bottom then add two inches of soft rock phosphate and a five-and-one-half-inch layer of a compost mixture. Then add two inches of a 50/50 mix of soft rock phosphate and sand. Plant potato pieces, each having two eyes, in the soft rock phosphate sand mixture, both preferably facing north. Cover this layer with four inches of compost, then two inches of straw. When the sprouts peak through the straw, cover with four more inches of straw and repeat this until the sprouts protrude out the top of the barrel. Allow the potato plant to grow in the barrel, watering and foliar spraying as needed, until harvest, when the barrel will be full of clean potatoes. Experiment with picking off the blossoms from the growing plants. This may increase tuber size. Oat straw is ideal, but wheat or rye will do nicely.

This next section is intended to give the reader a general overview of how commercial fertilizers are labeled and what the labeling means. When you purchase a bag of fertilizer, there will be analysis numbers on the bag. These numbers may be 18-3-3, 12-12-12, 20-3-15, etc. They refer respectively to the percentages of nitrogen (N), phosphate (P_2O_5), and potash (K_2O). Occasionally, there are more than three numbers on the bag; the fourth number refers to some other nutrient like calcium or sulfate. For example, ammonium sulfate has a label analysis of 21-0-0-26, meaning 21 percent nitrogen, 0 percent phosphate, 0 percent potash, and 26 percent sulfur. Calcium nitrate is 15-0-0-19 Ca, meaning 15 percent nitrogen, 0 percent phosphate, 0 percent potash, and 19 percent calcium.

Farmers and gardeners are sold fertilizers primarily on numbers or analysis with no consideration at all for quality. Consumers are told that fertilizer is fertilizer. This is as true as saying all gasoline and oil is the same, all steel is the same, or all cloth is the same.

The most common source of nitrogen in dry, bagged fertilizers is urea (46-0-0). It's cheap, but not generally preferred for progressive fertilization. Use the form of nitrogen best suited to the growth stage, such as nitrate or ammonia, in a form such as calcium nitrate, potassium nitrate, ammonium sulfate, household ammonia, or ammonium thiosulfate. The most common source of phosphate in dry bagged fertilizers is triple super phosphate (0-46-0). It's also cheap, and not preferred for progressive fertilization. It is too highly acidized and will quickly form insoluble compounds in the soil, thus rendering it useless. The most common source of potash in dry bagged fertilizers is muriate of potash, potassium chloride, 0-0-60 or 0-0-62, which has already been covered in detail. It is extremely deleterious to progressive fertilization.

All three of these products are inexpensive and have a high numerical analysis. It is argued that they supply the most plant food units for the dollar. To the uninformed purchaser this can be very convincing. Most states require a minimum of 24 total N-P-K units in order for the product to be registered for sale, that is, an analysis figure at or above 8-8-8. Anything less than a total of 24 units is usually not registerable as a fertilizer. The purpose of this regulation is to prevent many "organic" fertilizers and less concentrated products from being marketed. Consider the following comparison. A typical dry blend fertilizer with the analysis of 12-12-12 can be purchased for about $170 per ton. This product is made with the following materials:

> 523 pounds urea (46% N)
> 522 pounds triple-super-phosphate (46% P_2O_5)
> 400 pounds muriate of potash (60% K_2O)
> 556 pounds sand or dolomite filler
>
> ───────────────────────────────
>
> 2,000 pounds (rounded)

Here are 1,444 pounds of plant food and 556 pounds of a filler which is of no value or is a detriment — as is dolomite, for it is high in magnesium. (Note: The magnesium here will combine with the nitrogen, forming a magnesium nitrate salt that dehydrates and leaches the nitrogen out of the available nutrient system, thus, under this type of N-P-K system, creating a need for the purchaser to buy still more nitrogen.) In any event, 1,444 pounds of plant food at $170 per ton is $.118 per pound of plant food. Next, here is a typical "organic" fertilizer with the analysis of 4-4-2 that sells for $200 per ton. This product is made with the following materials:

> 81 pounds ammonium sulfate
> 364 pounds soft rock phosphate
> 80 pounds sulfate of potash
> 1,475 pounds compost blend
> ———————————————
> 2,000 pounds

What is unique about this product is that all 2,000 pounds of this ton is usable plant food. Therefore, the cost of $200 per ton amounts to only $.10 per pound of plant food. The greatest difference is that this product is beneficial and the first one is not. State agencies and universities are totally sympathetic to the chemical and fertilizer industries. The fertilizers on the market are designed to create an increased dependency on them, and on rescue chemicals to fight insect and disease infestations.

Fertilizer labeling is a political game. Though there are some basic guidelines and consistencies, by and large each state makes up its own rules. The basic affinity the states share is that they seek to protect the system and squelch true progress.

When a product does not fall into their definition of a fertilizer, it can possibly get registered as a soil amendment. The catch here is that the state's university must have first researched the product to show it has "merit," a costly process that eliminates the smaller companies. Chemistry has no bearing here. A prime example is humic acid. It is a proven fact that humic acid is eminently useful for solubilizing soil and plant nutrients, as any competent chemist can attest. There are several chemical companies that add humic acid to their herbicides to buffer the damage done to the crop it is used on, such as soybeans. Humic acid is not registerable as a soil amendment because ". . . our university hasn't researched it and proven its value." The companies, then, must adulterate the product by adding a random trace element and registering the product as a trace element in fertilizer such as calcium, manganese, or sulfur. This creates a facade. Another problem in marketing good products is that many state agencies will not recognize university research data from another state because they contend that their soil is different, as if biochemistry changes as soon as you cross a state line. Of course the soil conditions may vary, yet the principles of biochemistry and biophysics are the same whether you study at the University of Michigan or Stanford. If they weren't, how could you get an undergraduate degree in one state and a graduate degree in another?

DISEASES AND INSECTS VS. NUTRIENT DEFICIENCES

Diseases and insect infestations are nothing more than nature's way of saying there is a nutrient deficiency in the plants that makes them nutritionally unfit for higher forms of life to consume. Billions of dollars are spent every year on chemicals to fight diseases and insects, and consequently billions of dollars are spent on drugs and supplements for the consumers of this minerally deficient food. It is indeed a degenerative merry-go-round, but it is being rectified in many isolated areas by simple, common-sense fertilization. These practices could save billions in wasted expenditures, not to mention the health benefits that would be derived by all concerned.

The following is by no means an exhaustive list, yet it will give the reader an understanding of the cooperative structure of natural laws. The reader will also, upon reading, become more competent at understanding problems in his own backyard.

The bottom line is that until the cause behind the cause of the symptom is corrected, the symptom will return. The fungi, viruses, bacteria, and insects are only the garbage crew. You can correct the problem by eliminating the nutrient deficiency, beginning with the first nutrient listed and proceeding sequentially thereafter. Keep in mind that the rules of nature mentioned in this book remain constant throughout. Often when the first one, two, or three nutrients listed are supplied, the remaining nutrient deficiencies will follow suit without their actual application because the plant's magnetism and transmutative energy is usually sufficient to carry out the process. Remember the one key rule that all nutrients must be in phosphate form in order to be properly assimilated into a healthy biological system. Next is a list of these same crops with the corresponding Brix readings, at or above which there will be no disease, insect, nor malady infestation. They are the same for the plant as well as the fruit. Today, a significant contributor or outright cause to these nutrient deficiencies is the presence of glyphosate. This is discussed at length by Dr. Don Huber in his many presentations. As a strong chelator, glyphosate binds to cation nutrients, immobilizing them for nutritive functions. Even though the soil/tissue test may indicate adequate cation nutrient presence, glyphosate can inactivate these nutrients leaving the soil/tissue test useless.

INSECTS	SEQUENTIAL NUTRIENT DEFICIENCIES

Celery Insects

Aphids	Ca, P, Fe, Cu
Varigated Cutworm	Ca, P, Cu, Mn, vitamin C, vitamin E
Cabbage Looper	P, Ca, vitamin C, Fe
Carrot Weevil	Ca, P, vitamin A

Rose Insects

Aphids	Ca, P, Fe, Cu
Rose Chafer	Ca, P, Mn
Rose Midge	Ca, vitamin C (medium level deficiency)
Rose Stem Borer	Ca, vitamin C (high level deficiency)
Spider Mites	Ca, P, Fe/Cu
Thrips	Ca, P, Co
Leaf-Cutter Bees	Ca, P, Fe, Cu, Co/B (they will only nest in deficient plants)
Rose Galls	Ca, P, Fe/Cu, Co/B (they will only nest in deficient plants)
Rose Scale	Ca, P, vitamin C
Rose Slugs	Ca, P, Fe
Japanese Beetle	Ca, Cu

Strawberry Insects

Strawberry Weevil/Clipper	Ca, P, Fe, Cu
Strawberry Sap Beetle	Ca, P, Mn
Tarnished Plant or Lygus Bug	Ca, P, vitamin C, Mn
Spittlebugs	Ca, P, vitamin C, Fe
Strawberry Leafhopper	Ca, P, vitamin C, Co, Se
Flea Beetle	Ca, P, Fe/Cu

Strawberry Insects (continued)

Aphids	Ca, P, Fe/Cu
Mites	Ca, P
White Grubs	P, Ca, vitamin C, Mn, Co, Cu
Strawberry Rat Weevil	Ca, P, Se
Strawberry Rootworm	Ca, P, Fe/Cu, Co
Nematodes	Ca, P

Raspberry Insects

Fruitworm	Ca, P, vitamin C
Crown Borer	Ca, P, Co, vitamin C
Sawfly	Ca, P, Fe/Cu, vitamin C, Se
Cane Borer	Ca, P, vitamin C, vitamin E
Aphids	Ca, P, Fe, Cu
Mites	Ca, P

Potato Insects

White Grub	P, Ca, vitamin C, Mn, Co, Cu
Wire Worm	Ca, Co, vitamin C
Colorado Potato Beetle	Ca, P, vitamin C, Cu, Mn
Potato Leaf Hopper	Ca, P, Mn, Cu, Fe
Cabbage Looper	P, Ca, vitamin C, Fe
Variegated Cutworm	Ca, P, Cu, Mn, vitamin C, vitamin E
Green Peach Aphids	Ca, P, Cu, Fe
Potato Flea Beetle	vitamin C, Ca, P, Fe, vitamin E, Cu, Mn

Lettuce & Onion Insects

Aster Leaf Hopper (6-spotted)	Ca, P, Se
Green Peach Aphids	Ca, P, Cu, Fe
Onion Thrips	Ca, P, vitamin E
Onion Maggot	Ca, P, Co, vitamin C

Cucumber, Melon, Squash, & Pumpkin Insects

Seed Corn Maggot	Ca, P, carbohydrate, Cu
Spotted Cucumber Beetles	Ca, P, Fe, Cu
Onion Thrips	Ca, P, vitamin E
Striped Cucumber Beetles	Ca, P, vitamin C, Co
Green Peach Aphids	Ca, P, Cu, Fe

Tomato, Eggplant & Pepper Insects

Black Cutworm	Ca, P, Fe
Pepper Mosaic Disease	Ca, P
Flea Beetle	Ca, P, Se
Tomato Hornworm	Ca, P, Cu
Tobacco Hornworm	Ca, P, Co
Tomato Fruitworm	Ca, P, Se, Co
European Corn Borer	Ca, P
Corn Ear Worm	Ca, P, Mn

DISORDER OR DISEASE NAME	SYMPTOMATIC PATHOLOGY	SEQUENTIAL NUTRIENT DEFICIENCIES
Tomatoes		
Damping off	Fungi	Carbohydrate, Mn (sugar near seed, soak seed)
Collar Rot	Fungi	Ca, Cu
Anthracnose	Fungi	Ca, P, Cu
Septoria Leaf Spot	Fungus	Ca, P, vitamin C
Early Blight	Fungus	P, vitamin C
Late Blight	Fungus	P, vitamin C
Buckeye Rot	Fungus	Ca, P, Cu
Verticillium Wilt	Fungus	P, Cu, Mn
Fusarium Wilt	Fungus	P, Cu, Mo
Walnut/Butternut Wilt	Tree Excretion	P, Cu, vitamin C
Bacterial Canker/Wilt	Bacteria	P, Ca, Fe/Cu
Bacterial Speck	Bacteria	Ca, P, Mn, Fe/Cu (low level)
Bacterial Spot	Bacteria	Ca, P, Mn, Fe/Cu (high level)
Tomato Viruses	Viruses	Ca, P, vitamin C, Co, Se, vitamin E
Blossom End Rot	Moisture Stress	Ca, P, Mn/Cu (equally)
Catface	Abnormal Growing Conditions	K, P, Co
Sunscald	Excessive Sun	Ca, carbohydrate, beta carotene, vitamin C
Leaf Roll	Irregular Water Supply	Carbohydrate, Fe, Cu (salt excess)
Lightning Injury	Not considered	Soil has a lefthand noxious vortex caused by major soil imbalance which nature attempts to correct with lightning

DISORDER OR DISEASE NAME	SYMPTOMATIC PATHOLOGY	SEQUENTIAL NUTRIENT DEFICIENCIES
Tomatoes (continued)		
Growth Cracks	Rapid Growth	Carbohydrate, Cu, vitamin C
Blotchy Ripening	Adverse, Climate, Cultural & Nutritional Balances	Ca, P, K, Mn
Zippers	Another Malfunction Cold Weather	Mn, Cu, Ca, P
Blossom Drop	Climate Conditions, Weather, Poor Fertilization of Ovary	P, Ca, MN (nitrate nitrogen excess)

Potatoes

Leak	Fungus	Ca, P, B
Black Scurf	Fungus	Carbohydrate
Late Blight	Fungus	P, vitamin C
Common Scab	Bacteria	P
Silver Scurf	Fungus	Cu, Mo
Wilt	Fungus	P, Cu
Blackleg	Bacteria	Cu, B
Ring Rot	Bacteria	Ca, P
Soft Rot	Bacteria	Ca, K, B
Dry Rot	Fungus	Ca, Co
Early Blight	Fungus	P, vitamin C
Potato Leaf Roll	Virus	P, Ca, Cu

Alfalfa

Common Leaf Spot	Fungus	P, Ca (spots from potash excess, yellow due to either magnesium excess or nitrogen deficiency which excess magnesium causes)
Yellow Leaf Blotch	Fungus	P, Ca, N
Leptosphaerulina Leaf Spot	Fungus	P, Ca, vitamin C, vitamin E
Stemphylium Leaf Spot	Fungus	P, Ca, Co, vitamin C, vitamin E
Summer Black Stem & Leaf Spot	Fungus	P, Ca, carbohydrate, Cu, Fe/Zn

DISORDER OR DISEASE NAME	SYMPTOMATIC PATHOLOGY	SEQUENTIAL NUTRIENT DEFICIENCIES

Alfalfa (continued)

Rust	Fungus	P, Ca, vitamin A, Co
Downy Mildew	Fungus	P, Ca, vitamin C, Cu, Fe
Alfalfa Mosiac	Virus	P, Ca, vitamin C, iron, Co
Bacterial Leaf Spot	Bacteria	Ca, vitamin C, N, P (2nd is potash excess)
Spring Black Stem	Fungus	P, Ca, Fe, Co, vtiamin C
Cerospora Leaf Spot	Fungus	P, Ca, carbohydrate, Cu, Fe/Zn
Bacterial Wilt	Bacteria	P, Ca, vitamin C, Fe/Cu, Se/Co, vitamin A
Phytophthora Root Rot	Fungus	P, Ca, B, vitamin C
Anthracnose	Fungus	P, Ca, vitamin C
Fusarium Crown Rot	Fungus	P, Ca, Cu, Fe, Mo
Mycoleptodiscus Crown Rot	Fungus	P, Ca, carbohydrate, vitamin C
Sclerotina Crown & Stem Rot	Fungus	P, Ca, vitamin C, Cu, Fe
Fusarium Wilt	Fungus	Ca, Cu, P, Fe, Mo
Rhizoctonia Stem Canker	Fungus	P, Ca, vitamin C, Fe/Cu
Violet Root Rot	Fungus	P, Ca, Co
Crown Wart	Fungus	P, Ca, vitamin C, vitamin E
Dodder	Parasitic Weed	P, Ca, Fe

Raspberries

Mosaic Virus	Virus	Ca, P, Fe, Cu
Leaf Curl Virus	Virus	Ca, P, vitamin E
Toabcco Streak Virus	Virus	Ca, P, Fe, Mo
Tomato Ringspot Virus	Virus	Ca, P, vitamin C, Fe, vitamin A
Anthracnose	Fungus	Ca, P, Fe
Spur Blight	Fungus	Ca, P, vitamin C, Se
Cane Blight	Fungus	P, vitamin C, Se
Orange Rust	Fungus	Ca, P, vitamin C (early-season deficiency)
Late Leaf Rust	Fungus	Ca, P, vitamin C (late-season deficiency)
Verticillium Wilt	Fungus	Ca, P, Co
Phytophthora Root Rot	Fungus	Ca, Se, P
Botrytis	Fungus/Mold	Ca, P, Co, vitamin C

DISORDER OR DISEASE NAME	SYMPTOMATIC PATHOLOGY	SEQUENTIAL NUTRIENT DEFICIENCIES
Raspberries (continued)		
Pennicillium	Fungus/Mold	Ca, P, Se
Crown Gall	Bacteria	Ca, P, Fe/Cu, vitamin C
Cane Gall	Bacteria	Ca, P, Mo
Blueberries		
Mummyberry	Fungus	Ca, P, Mn
Fusicoccum Canker	Fungus	Ca, P, Co, Se
Phomopsis Canker	Fungus	Ca, P, vitamin C, Co
Botrytis Blight	Fungus	Ca, P, vitamin C (early-season deficiency)
Anthracnose	Fungus	Ca, P, Co, Mn (early-season deficiency)
Alternaria Fruit Rot	Fungus	Ca, P, Co, Mn (late-season deficiency)
Red Leaf Disease	Fungus	Ca, P, Co, Fe/Cu, Se
Powdery Mildew	Fungus	Ca, P, vitamin C (mid- to late-season deficiency)
Crown Gall	Bacteria	Ca, P
Shoestring	Virus	Ca, P, Fe/Cu, Co
Necrotic Ringspot	Virus	Ca, P, carbohydrate
Blueberry Leaf Mottle	Virus	Ca, P, Fe/Cu, Se
Mosaic	Virus	P, Ca, Fe
Red Ringspot	Virus	Ca, P, Co, Se
Stunt	Virus	Ca, P, carbohydrate, Co
Roses		
Black spot	Fungus	Ca, Cu, Fe
Cankers	Fungus	Ca, sulfate (gypsum lime $CaSO_4$)
Crown Gall	Bacteria	Ca, P, vitamin C, Co
Powdery Mildew	Fungus	Ca, vitamin A
Rust	Fungus	Ca, vitamin C, Se
Viruses	Virus	Ca, P, Mn

DISORDER OR DISEASE NAME	SYMPTOMATIC PATHOLOGY	SEQUENTIAL NUTRIENT DEFICIENCIES
Strawberries		
Verticillium Wilt	Fungus	P, Cu, Mn
Red Stele	Fungus	P, Cu, Fe
Black Root Rot	Unknown	Ca, P, vitamin C
Grey Mold	Fungus	Ca, P
Stem End Rot	Fungus	Ca, P, vitamin C, Mn
Leather Rot	Fungus	Ca, P, Mn, Co
Leaf Scorch	Fungus	Ca, P, Co, Se
Leaf Blight	Fungus	Ca, P, N, vitamin C
Leaf Spot	Fungus	Ca, P, Se
Powdery Mildew	Fungus	Ca, P, vitamin C, Co
Viruses	Virus	Ca, P, vitamin C, Co, Se, vitamin E
Cucumber, Melon, Squash, Pumpkin		
Bacterial Wilt	Bacteria	Ca, P, vitamin C
Cucumber Mosaic	Virus	Ca, P
Celery		
Late Blight	Fungus	P, vitamin C
Early Blight	Fungus	P, vitamin C
Bacterial Blight	Bacteria	P, Cu/Fe, vitamin C
Sclerotina Rot	Fungus	Ca, P, vitamin C, Fe, Co
Damping Off	Fungus	P, Ca, vitamin C, Mo
Crater Rot	Fungus	Ca, P, Se, Fe, vitamin E
Fusarium Yellows	Fungus	Ca, P, Cu, Fe
Cucumber Mosaic	Virus	Ca, P, vitamin C, vitamin E, Se
Common Celery Mosaic	Virus	Ca, P, vitamin C, Co, Se
Aster Yellows	Virus	Ca, P, vitamin E, Fe, Cu
Black Heart	Rapid Growth	Ca, P, B, Co
Cracked Stem	Boron Deficiency	Ca, P, vitamin A (boron acts as a growth inhibitor and by slowing the growth the plant uses and requires less of the three nutrients thus the symptom of cracked stem disappears)

DISORDER OR DISEASE NAME	SYMPTOMATIC PATHOLOGY	SEQUENTIAL NUTRIENT DEFICIENCIES
Corn		
Corn Smut	Fungus	Ca, P
Yellow Leaf Blight	Fungus	Ca, P, Se
Northern Corn Leaf Blight	Fungus	Ca, P, Fe
Kernel Red Streak	Wheat Curl Mite Toxin	Genetic, not detrimental, reverting back to native gene
Diplodia Ear Rot	Fungus	Ca, P
Anthracnose	Fungus	Ca, P, Fe/Cu, Co (testimony)

Apples		
Northwestern Anthracnose or Bull's Eye Rot	Fungus	Ca, P, vitamin C, Co
Bitter Rot	Fungus	Ca, P, vitamin C
Botrytis Rot	Fungus	Ca, P, Co, vitamin C
Black Rot or Frogeye Leaf Spot	Fungus	Ca, P, Co
Sooty Blotch & Fly Speck	Fungus	Ca, P, Fe/Cu
Soft Rot or Blue Mold Rot	Fungus	Ca, P, Se, Co
Internal Breakdown	Old age	Ca, P, vitamin C, Fe/Cu
Apple Scab	Fungus	Ca, Fe/Cu, P
Soft Scald	Poor conditions	Ca, P, Mo
Cedar Apple Rust	Fungus	Ca, P, Fe/Cu, Co
Quince Rust	Fungus	Ca, P, Mn
Nectria Canker	Fungus	Ca, P, vitamin C, Fe/Cu (high level deficiency)
Papery Bark Canker	Fungus	Ca, P, carbohydrate, Co
Botryosphaeria Rot	Fungus	Ca, P, Co
Bitter Pit or Jonathan Spot	Water supply	Ca, P, Mn, Co
Powdery Mildew	Fungus	Ca, P, Fe/Cu
Phytophthora Collar Rot	Fungus	Ca, P, Se, Mo
Water Core	Environment	Ca, P, Fe/Cu, Mn
Fire Blight	Bacteria	Ca, P, vitamin C
Brown Rot	Fungus	Ca, P, Co, vitamin C

DISORDER OR DISEASE NAME	SYMPTOMATIC PATHOLOGY	SEQUENTIAL NUTRIENT DEFICIENCIES
Apples (continued)		
Apple Mosaic	Virus	Ca, P, Se
Trunk Twisting & Flattening	Virus	Ca, P
Russet Ring	Virus	Ca, P, Fe
Leaf Pucker	Virus	Ca, P, Mo
2,4-D Injury		P, if the Brix reading is high enough (14+), the tree won't "pick up" the 2,4-D to begin with
Brown Heart or Core	Cold storage	Ca, P, often corresponds with trunk twisting and flattening

Minimum Brix Reading

(At which and above *no* disease, insect, or malady will infest.)

Strawberries	16
Raspberries	15
Blueberries	14
Alfalfa	14
Roses	15
Tomatoes	18
Potatoes	13
Cucumbers	13
Melons	16
Squash	15
Pumpkin	15
Lettuce	12
Onion	13
Celery	15
Apples	16
Field Corn (Yellow)	12
Field Corn (White)	13
Sweet Corn (Yellow)	23
Sweet Corn (White)	24
Sweet Cherries	16
Sour Cherries	14
Beans	14
Peas	14
Eggplant	12
Pepper	12

After reading the disease and insect charts, you should notice several patterns. The insects carry the same deficiencies regardless of the plant infested. Even though the pattern is similar, however, the diseases indicate slightly different specific deficiencies for each plant infected. Also, many diseases indicate the same mineral deficiencies. The difference is that one disease manifests itself early in the season while the other manifests itself late in the season, depending on whether the deficiencies appear early or late.

Notice how often calcium and phosphate show up as number one or two deficiencies, yet are the least recommended nutrients by conventional soil scientists. Notice also how infrequently nitrogen and potash show up as deficiencies even though they are the nutrients most frequently recommended by conventional soil scientists.

You will recall that typical soil scientists recommend calcium by pH and recommend phosphate according to a standard norm rather than refractometer readings. The conventional correction of all infestations is to spray with a poisonous chemical rather than correcting the nutrient deficiency. There is more money in this approach for the chemical petroleum syndicate, because the infestations will always reappear later or during the next year, warranting more poisonous chemicals.

Look at the chart on blueberries and note that all the disease symptoms list calcium and phosphate as the first two nutrient deficiencies. It is interesting that the experts almost always scorn calcium and phosphate for use on blueberries, especially calcium. They mouth the pH argument and contend that blueberries won't thrive unless the soil is sour (has a low pH). The actual situation is that because there is a deficiency of available phosphate, the nutrients, especially the heavy trace elements, are in competition for the phosphate carrier. When the pH is lowered, the resistance in the soil is lowered. Therefore the heavier traces can better compete for the limited phosphate at the expense of other elements. Nature always follows the line of least resistance. If it were not for some of these heavier elements getting into the plant, no blueberry plant would ever grow, precisely the case in mid- to high-pH soils, due to the phosphate deficiency. Again, the answer is simple. Provide adequate calcium and especially phosphate to achieve the minimum Brix readings listed on the chart and no pathologies or insect infestations will occur. With ideal nutrient balances, the ideal soil pH for all soils and all crops is 6.4. Remember that natural laws remain constant and consistent; pH is a trailing indicator, an effect, not a cause. Balance the nutrients and let the pH fall where it may.

Another interesting phenomenon indicated by these charts is a frequent deficiency of cobalt and selenium. Michigan and other states have long been known for their deficiencies in these elements, yet they are not recognized as fertilizer components and are almost never recommended for plant feeding. There is more profit in adding these elements continuously to animal feeds and drugging the animals and people for the symptom developed as a result of their absence.

One will also notice frequent vitamin deficiencies, especially of vitamin C. Vitamin C is extremely important for calcium assimilation, as well as several other functions in living organisms. Vitamins are also not recognized by the "experts" as fertilizer components.

Carbohydrates are deficient in seed maladies or whenever the system runs out of energy. Carbohydrates are manufactured during photosynthesis for energy storage, and their manufacture is dependent upon phosphate. Often molasses or Clintose corn sugar are applied to boost the carbohydrate balance. Again, this strategy is not recognized by the experts, yet it works.

Fortunately, we live in a country where the spirit of independence still exists, and there are those who not only question the system but are proving it false by exemplifying the truth. This is done by growing plants at or above minimum Brix values and observing that they are completely free of all the maladies and infestations that plague the conventional system. The problem is that the system sets standards according to perceived norms, and its definition of normal assumes that weeds, diseases, and insects attack regardless of quality. This observation is correct only within the parameters of the spray and kill system.

When foods and crops are passed off as being "disease free" after they have been bombarded by poisonous chemicals to kill the symptomatic pathogen, the mineral deficiency that attracted the pathogen in the first place still exists. When the food is deficient, the consumer will be correspondingly deficient.

An analogy could be made to an automobile engine. Engines are equipped with a gasoline filter and an air filter. One can remove both and the engine will continue to function. But for how long, and at what efficiency will it function? How many nagging problems will develop along the way and what condition will the engine be in at trade-in time, if it makes it that long? It is doubtful that it would be worth overhauling.

Insects and diseases are the filter system in the food chain to keep the junk and garbage away from the consumers. Modern agriculture has substituted poisonous chemicals for this natural filtering system. How ingenious. You need not investigate long to realize that the magnitude of the danger caused by agriculture chemicals is enormous. Chemicals such as Parathion and Temik (aldicarb) are highly toxic and used frequently by vegetable growers. These chemicals are lethal and are polluting the water, soils, and food chain. Electronic scanner analysis proves this beyond any doubt. Of course, the chemical syndicate and the universities deny this. What people don't know won't hurt them, right? The crucial fact is that these lethal chemicals are not needed to begin with because the problem is deficient soil fertility. Correct it and not only will the need for chemicals disappear, but nature will then have the capacity to clean up what has already been applied. When analyzed by electronic scanners, plants that have high Brix readings do not contain detectable levels of toxic chemicals, nor do the soils they are grown in, despite the fact that chemicals were previously applied. Likewise, plants that have low Brix readings do contain detectable levels of toxic chemicals, as do the soils they were grown in/on, in some cases even if no toxic chemicals were applied.

In fairness it is important to mention that not all university research and teaching is as wasteful or as futile as this aspect of agriculture. The guilty party is mainly that part of the system tied to the chemical fertilizer syndicate and kingpinned by the petroleum industry. There are people like Dr. Philip Callahan, who is a retired USDA entomologist, who have proven that insects and diseases are indicators of mineral deficiencies. There is Dr. Don Huber, a retired plant pathologist from Purdue University, who is revealing the truth about glyphosate. There is Allan Savory, a conventional African biologist for years who finally realized the error of his ways and pioneered "mob grazing" or intensive grazing as *the* way to regenerate desert around the world. There is Michael McNeill, a former USDA soil and genetics researcher, who left the USDA to start his own independent research station and consulting business in biological agriculture. He is one of a handful of world experts in soybean rust and fungal diseases in crops. As more of these true scientists appear, and as the public demands quality in its foodstuffs, a copacetic situation free of pollution, dangerous chemicals, and toxic waste accidents will evolve.

The garden section would not be complete without the discussion of the birds and the bees, boys and girls. Most people believe that they understand the difference between boys and girls; however, when asked to correlate that "understanding" to plants in the garden, they are stumped. Plants have male and female aspects. Garden plants harvested for their foliage or florets are "male" and those harvested for their seed or fruit are "female." Most gardeners have had seasons where their tomato plants, melon plants, cucumber plants, or okra plants grew wonderfully, but they didn't harvest much fruit. They blamed everything from the weather to the seed variety to God for the problem. The truth was just a lack of understanding about "boys" and "girls."

In this case, there was too much "male" energy in the garden, meaning too much nitrate nitrogen and probably potassium as well, knowing how most gardeners fertilize their soils. What was missing was enough "female" energy to switch the plants to seed or fruit production. This is generally easily done with a foliar spray or two. This is a deficiency of ammonia nitrogen, phosphate, manganese, sulfur, and other trace minerals.

A very fun and practical foliar spray to apply in this situation is the following:
- 1 quart spray bottle — fill half full with purified water.
- 6 ounces of Coca-Cola — yes, the real thing, not diet. It contains carbon dioxide, which plants love; sugar to feed the microbes on the leaf; phosphoric acid, which the plant needs; and caffeine, which induces protein synthesis/manufacturing in the plant.
- 1 to 3 tablespoons of apple cider vinegar

- 1 to 2 tablespoons of household ammonia — yes, that you use to mop the floors.
- 1 to 3 tablespoons of sea water or 10 to 30 trace mineral drops or "Alka Trace"

Add more water to the mix to completely fill the quart bottle, mix gently and mist your plants in the early evening, preferably after 8:00 pm. Mist just enough that you see mist on the leaves but not so much as the leaves are drenched and dripping profusely. This spray can be given every two to seven days until fruit begins to set or can be continued through the rest of the season. If still after a couple weeks you don't get fruit set, then add another tablespoon of vinegar. For this to work best there must be adequate calcium in the soil. Adding a gallon or two of whole milk to the soil per week depending upon the size of the garden can be beneficial and add precious available calcium and foods for beneficial microbes.

Chapter 6

Quality Produce

Have you ever purchased what looked like good quality fresh vegetables, put them in your refrigerator, only to throw them in the garbage three days later because they had spoiled? Have you purchased fresh vegetables or fruits and discovered that several weeks later they were only slightly dehydrated yet perfectly good to eat? High-quality produce, in the true sense of the word, will not rot. It will simply dehydrate with age. For some, this is a very difficult statement to acknowledge, since the majority of the produce in this county does rot if not consumed a few days after purchase. We are told that the quality of produce can be verified by its looks (apples are coated with wax so they shine, lettuce is coated with sulfide so it remains green, meat is treated with nitrates so it remains red) and the lack of visual signs of insects and diseases. Little is said about the spectrum of rescue chemicals applied to produce the false visual perfection. The culprit here is the myth that insect and disease infestation is indiscriminate as to crop quality. Conventional agricultural scientists contend that crops, weeds, insects, and diseases are all competitive. In a balanced biological system this could not be further from the truth.

Weeds grow where the soil is balanced for them rather than for the cultivated crops. Insects and diseases infect those plants that are of such poor quality that they aren't fit for higher life forms to eat.

Unfortunately, modern agriculture has opted to ignore this is basic biological law and flood the market with produce of false quality.

How can you determine, then, the true quality of produce? You need a method or tool, and then a standard with which to make comparisons. Currently the refractometer is the most practical tool that the average person can use to evaluate produce quality.

The refractometer is a tool that measures the refractive index of a liquid. When light rays shine through the liquid they strike the carbohydrate, salt, and other molecules depending upon the type of calibration used. When the light rays strike the molecules, they bend or refract. The greater the calibrated molecular concentration of the liquid in question, the greater the refraction.

Refractometers are used extensively in industry and research fields for measuring the concentration of all kinds of aqueous solutions such as pharmaceuticals, tissue fluids in plants, and urine and blood protein. It is also used for checking the concentration of medicines, cosmetics, battery solutions, anti-freeze, and processing solutions for plating, and quenching oils.

The food processing industry uses the refractometer extensively for measuring the sugar concentration of soft drinks, juices, colas, nectars, and lactic acid beverages. The device is also used for checking flavoring solutions of canned foods, sugar concentration of jams, marmalades, honeys, syrups, extracts, concentrates, and other sweet liquids. Refractometers are used in the brewing and wine-making industry as well.

The refractometers to use for quality control in crop field production should be calibrated from 0 to 30 or 32 Brix, to measure sucrose. The irony here is that the use of refractometers has been known and practiced by the industry for decades, and yet if you were to inquire at the local cooperative extension service about using a refractometer for monitoring crop quality and selecting various feeds and fertilizers, you would get something between a blank stare and arrogant dismissal of your question. In certain parts of the country refractometers are used by farmers to check the ripening stage of fruit and the sugar content of fruits and grapes, but for various reasons very few farmers have adopted the extensive use of these instruments for improving the crop quality, not just measuring its status. Even fewer users of the device have noticed and correlated its readings to insect and disease, infestations, mineral content, shelf life, crop vigor, palatability, and chemical contamination.

Checking produce with a refractometer is quite simple and can be done in a matter of minutes.

First, check the refractometer's calibration. This is done by placing a drop or two of distilled water on the glass prism. Close the plate and look through the eyepiece. Focus, if possible, so that a clear distinction can be seen between the white field of view and the colored, usually blue, field. The distinct edge between the two colors is where the value on the scale is read. It should be at zero for distilled water. Adjust the calibration screw accordingly.

It is not imperative that you carry around distilled water just to calibrate the refractometer each time you use it, unless you plan to compare the readings with readings taken after calibration. In other words, if you are selecting produce from a farm market and plan to purchase the best of three samples, the actual reading can be plus or minus several points due to calibration error and still give accurate comparative information because all three sample tests would have the same error. You should simply purchase the produce with the highest reading between the three.

To test the produce, place one or two drops of juice on the glass prism, close the plate and look through the eye piece. It may be necessary to point the refractometer toward a light so the field of view is more distinct.

As a broad generalization, produce over 12 Brix is considered good because crops above this value are usually not bothered by insects or diseases, so the produce will be fit for human and animal consumption according to the law of natural selection. Keep in mind that this 12 Brix is from the weakest part of the fresh plant, 24-7. In other words, if we check sweet corn and the ear is 24 but it is still infested with ear worms, one will find that the stalk opposite the ear shank will have a Brix less than 12. Further, understand that the longer fruit and vegetables sit around after harvest the more they dehydrate. This dehydration will result in a higher Brix reading so one can be deceived into thinking this is an excellent fruit/vegetable. The reading at time of harvest is the more correct indicator of absolute quality.

For quite some time we believed that, if an item reads greater than 12, and if the distinction between the two colors in the field of view is unclear and difficult to pinpoint, it is an indication that this item is relatively high in calcium, a desirable condition. This is not necessarily true. Years of testing has shown that there can be a "fuzzy" line on the refractometer at a Brix of 1 for sap or fruit juice. Chlorophyll is the most common reason for a "fuzzy" line, not necessarily calcium.

It is possible, though not very common, to get a relatively high Brix reading with the refractometer and not have a premium quality item. Probably the most common occurrence of this is when sweet corn ready for harvest has a high Brix reading in the ear though it is infested with corn ear worms. If you monitor this corn for the entire season, you will see that the Brix reading is low and only at the end of the season does the plant translocate as much sugar as it can to the ear, thus raising the ear Brix reading. However, since the Brix reading was low throughout the growing season, the plant was nutritionally deficient and despite the last minute translocation of sugar to the ear, the mineral did not accompany this sugar. This phenomenon has been bred into many crops in an attempt to get the frosting without the cake, so to speak. The insects are not fooled at all. Another time when Brix readings may be high without really indicating a high mineral content is in a dehydrated condition such as a drought. If the produce rots or requires rescue chemicals to protect it from pests, then it is not really minerally enriched.

Evaluating produce with a refractometer is an enlightening experience. Cosmetic visual signs often crumble in the wake of real evaluation. As you practice at it, you will learn to discern cosmetic signs and signs of true natural quality. And parents will notice that fruits and vegetables shunned by fussy eaters are suddenly popular when the Brix readings fall into the good to excellent range.

The refractometer has virtually unlimited uses. The key to its value is keeping records and references. Record when and where a very poor or exceptionally good item is obtained, what it looks and tastes like, how it stores and cooks, and how it satisfies your hunger.

Figure 7

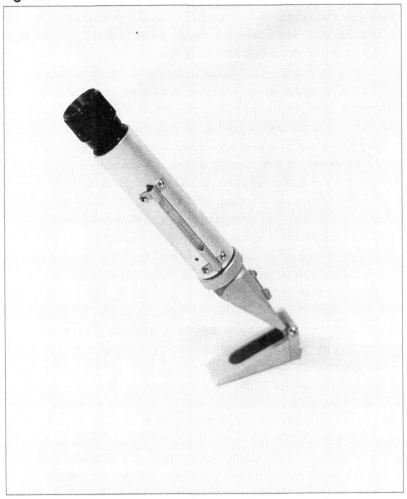

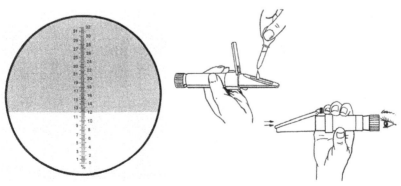

The refractometer can be used for fertilizer selection, large or small scale food evaluation (even milk), food processing, and a variety of other uses. Use it whenever and wherever the occasion arises.

The refractometer is only a tool. It must be used to be of any value, and the values you obtain from the instrument are only as good as their application. When it is used to compile trivial information, that will be its value. But when it is used as a tool to select the most nutritious produce to eat, then its value is priceless because good health is priceless, especially once it has escaped us.

Discussion of a tool is futile unless you are able to obtain one, so here are the names of three brands I am familiar with: Atago Model N1, American Optical, and Extech. There are many others of equal quality and comparable price. Plan to spend between $100 and $250 for a refractometer that should last indefinitely with proper care. If you are unable to locate a refractometer in your area, one can be purchased from Pike Agri-Lab Supplies, Inc., 154 Claybrook Road, P.O. Box 67, Jay, Maine 04239, phone (207) 897-9267, fax (207) 897-9268, www.pikeagri.com. I am not associated, but simply provide the contact for the reader's convenience. I wish you successful shopping and improved health as a result.

In addition to refractometer readings, there are visual characteristics you can look for when selecting produce. Pears, for example, should be squarish rather than conical in shape. Oranges should have a five-star calyx on the blossom end. Citrus should have thin skins. Potatoes should not have sunken eyes. Corn should not dent at maturity. Again, the most important aspect of produce quality is that the produce should not spoil or rot. Purchase items that are the heaviest per unit volume. Your scrutiny will be rewarded by more nutrition per dollar spent.

REFRACTIVE INDEX OF CROP JUICES
Calibrated in % Sucrose or Degree Brix

	Poor	Excellent
FRUITS		
Apples	6	18
Avocados	4	12
Bananas	8	14

REFRACTIVE INDEX OF CROP JUICES *continued*

	Poor	Excellent
Cantaloupe	8	16
Casaba	8	14
Cherries	6	16
Coconut	8	14
Grapes	8	24
Grapefruit	6	18
Honeydew	8	14
Kumquat	4	12
Lemons	4	12
Limes	4	12
Mangos	4	14
Oranges	6	20
Papayas	6	22
Peaches	6	18
Pears	6	14
Pineapple	12	22
Raisins	60	80
Raspberries	6	15
Strawberries	6	16
Tomatoes	4	18
Watermelon	8	16

VEGETABLES

	Poor	Excellent
Asparagus	2	12
Beets	2	12
Bell Peppers	4	12
Broccoli	6	12
Cabbage	6	12
Carrots	4	18
Cauliflower	4	12
Celery	4	12
Corn Stalks	4	20
Corn, young	6	24
Cow Peas	4	12
Endive	4	12

	Poor	Excellent
English Peas	8	14
Escarole	4	12
Field Peas	4	12
Green Beans	4	14
Hot Peppers	4	12
Kohlrabi	6	12
Lettuce	4	12
Onions	4	13
Parsley	4	12
Peanuts	4	12
Potatoes, Irish	3	7
Potatoes, Red	3	7
Potatoes, Sweet	6	14
Romaine	4	12
Rutabagas	4	12
Squash	6	14
Sweet Corn	6	24
Turnips	4	12

For reference, pure water has a reading of "0."

Within a given species of plant, the crop with the higher refractive index will have a higher sugar content, higher mineral content, higher protein content, and a greater specific gravity or density. This adds up to a sweeter tasting, more minerally nutritious food with a lower nitrate and water content and better storage characteristics. It will produce more alcohol from fermented sugars and be more resistant to insects, thus resulting in a decreased insecticide usage. Crops with a high sugar content will have a lower freezing point, and therefore be less prone to frost damage. Soil fertility needs may also be ascertained from this reading.

REFRACTIVE INDEX OF CROP JUICES
Calibrated in % Sucrose or Degree Brix

	Poor	Avg	Good	Excellent
Alfalfa	4	8	16	22
Apples	6	10	14	18
Asparagus	2	4	6	12
Avocados	4	6	8	12
Bananas	8	10	12	16
Beets	6	8	10	12
Bell Peppers	4	6	8	12
Broccoli	6	8	10	12
Cabbage	6	8	10	12
Carrots	4	6	12	18
Cantaloupe	8	12	14	16
Casaba	8	10	12	14
Cauliflower	4	6	8	12
Celery	4	6	10	12
Cherries	6	8	14	16
Coconut	8	10	12	14
Corn Stalks	4	8	14	20
Corn, young	6	10	18	24
Cow Peas	4	6	10	12
Cumquat	4	6	8	12
Endive	4	6	8	12
English Peas	8	10	12	14
Escarole	4	6	8	12
Field Peas	4	6	10	12
Grains	6	10	14	18
Grapes	8	12	16	20
Grapefruit	6	10	14	18
Green Beans	4	6	8	14
Honeydew	8	10	12	14
Hot Peppers	4	6	8	12
Kohlrabi	6	8	10	12
Lemons	4	6	8	12
Lettuce	4	6	8	12
Limes	4	6	10	12

REFRACTIVE INDEX OF CROP JUICES *continued*

	Poor	Avg	Good	Excellent
Mangos	4	6	10	14
Onions	4	6	8	13
Oranges	6	10	16	20
Papayas	6	10	18	22
Parsley	4	6	8	12
Peaches	6	10	14	18
Peanuts	4	6	8	12
Pears	6	10	12	14
Pineapple	12	14	20	22
Raisins	60	70	75	80
Raspberries	6	8	12	14
Romaine	4	6	8	12
Rutabagas	4	6	10	12
Sorghum	6	10	22	30
Squash	6	8	12	14
Strawberries	6	10	14	16
Sweet Corn	6	10	18	24
Sweet Potato	6	8	10	14
Tomatoes	4	6	8	12
Turnips	4	6	8	12
Watermelon	8	12	14	16

Chapter 7

Consumer Nutrition

Nutrition. Is nutrition a state of health, a state of nutrient balance, a fact, or an opinion? There are volumes and volumes of printed material on nutrition. Often this information is contradictory even though it is founded on numerous test cases and years of research. As with statistics in all fields, statistics on nutritional research can be arranged and emphasized to support numerous contentions and positions even if they are contradictory. It is common practice to research, test, and record statistical information on a given topic to support a predetermined position or contention to sell a given product, a belief, or a service, or to discredit another person's position. The important thing is to avoid the junk that detracts from health and to pursue the blessings that perpetuate health.

The modern food production system carries out quality control using a cosmetic approach. Crops are sprayed systematically to ward off insects and diseases. The crop is then harvested, processed with preservatives, injected, sprayed, or covered with wax for marketing purposes. The consumer is blasted with the idea that she is consuming high-quality food. It is analogous to purchasing a car that is rusted out but painted over, has worn-out engine and interior, but, since the outside looks nice from a quick paint job, is passed off as a good buy. It is often contended that if you eat a balanced diet, with something from all the food groups, then you will be healthy. Unfortunately there is no way to make something from nothing. If the food does not contain the proper nutrients, then the consumer will not receive those nutrients no matter how much he eats. Nutritional programs are not so bad in and of themselves. The primary problem with most is that they do not consider the fact of nutritionally deficient food that often contains many things it should not. The lower the quality of Brix measurement, the greater the chance that the food stuff contains something it should not, such as chemicals, drugs, heavy metals, or pathogens. An article in *Energy Healing* discussed the drug stilbestrol. This drug is used to accelerate the fattening of beef animals. It is now banned in this country but not in many of the countries that export beef to the United States. According to the article, this drug has been traced to people who suffer from obesity.

There have been many investigations of the repercussions from using antibiotics in animal feeds. A September 6, 1984, article in the *New England Journal of Medicine* says that the transmission of resistant bacteria to consumers is a topic of major concern. The Centers for Disease Control and Prevention's 2013 report "Antibiotic Resistance Threats in the United States" revealed that at least 2 million people a year become infected with antibiotic-resistant bacteria in the United States alone. Around 23,000 Americans die as a result of these infections each year. Private research has shown that agricultural chemicals are being passed to consumers through the water, crops, and drift. These chemicals in and of themselves are extremely toxic and inflict stress on biological life. And when two or more combine the result in some cases is an even more toxic compound. Often it is claimed that contamination of the environment, especially the crops themselves, is insignificant. The risk of contamination is easily glossed over when the lower limit of the test measurement is so high that low levels of toxins are not discovered. You won't find something you're not looking for. The whole situation boils down to this: Improve the quality of the crops and toxic chemicals will be totally unnecessary. When you eat a truly balanced diet, you will obtain the nutrients necessary for health. No one disputes that the incidence of terminal diseases is growing. It does not help the problem to bicker over trivial causes such as chemicals or pollution when they are only symptoms of the problem. You are only as nutritionally sound as the food you consume. Spraying a crop to kill a disease does not mean the crop is free of disease. It only means that the disease symptom will disappear until the chemical wears off. Correct the soil fertility imbalance and the nutritional problems of this planet will take care of themselves along with the pollution problems.

The war on nature and our food has not slowed from 1989 to 2014. It has in fact accelerated. Both attributed to and paralleling this accelerated assault on our food is the increase in both human and animal chronic disease, infertility, birth defects, behavior and learning problems (most notably autism), and resistant new and emerging infective organisms and agents as well as the number of disabled and debilitated people. Today we have a generation born that is expected to have a shorter life span than its parents, something unprecedented and unimaginable 30 years ago.

Chapter 8

Let's Eat!

Things have gotten a bit more complicated since the first edition of this book with regards to foods — unfortunately, not for the better. Even organics today in some cases are contaminated with glyphosate because of the residue still remaining in the soils for years, perhaps decades, after the last application. I recommend Organic Valley dairy products because, thanks to Paul Dettloff, DVM, they have the highest quality standards and demand farmers work on increasing their pasture Brix readings with appropriate soil fertility. Organic Valley is also encouraging their dairy farmers to convert their herds to A2/A2 cows. No other organization in the dairy world is doing that. As you read the following recipes, keep in mind that today we must ensure that the ingredients, such as soy and corn, are GMO free.

Eating is meant to be a blessing and a joy. You need not feel guilty nor fearful. Food is meant to enhance your health, not detract from it. The following are a few recipes that you may choose to use. Enjoy!

CAROB CANDY

3 tbsp sesame seed
3 tbsp soy powder
safflower oil
1/2 tsp vanilla

3 tbsp rice polish
1-3 tbsp carob powder
honey

Thoroughly mix the dry ingredients. Add enough oil and honey to sweeten and knead into a large ball. Form into small balls and roll in nuts, sunflower seeds, or coconut. Optional additions: 1 tbsp fresh wheat germ, 1 tbsp brewer's yeast, 1 tbsp whey, 1 tbsp bone meal powder, 1 tbsp rosehip powder, 1 tbsp papaya powder, 1 tbsp molasses. This recipe is very delicious and beneficial. Make only enough to eat at one time, for it does not store well. Leftovers are not usually a problem, however.

EGGPLANT CASSEROLE

Start by peeling the eggplants just under the skin and cut into 1" pieces. Soak in 1/4 cup salt to 1/2 gallon of distilled water for 20 to 30 minutes. The water will get dirty and should be discarded after soaking. Use non-iodized salt. Rinse with fresh water after soaking to remove any excessive salt or debris. Next put into a blender with enough water so pieces will blend. Do not completely liquefy, rather chop finely. Add remaining ingredients and simmer for 20 to 30 minutes, cool and serve.

You may dice an onion or chives or sprinkle with wheat germ over the top.

5 eggplants	1/2 cup canned
1/8 cup molasses	evaporated milk
1 tsp Cornucopia	or soy milk
"All Spices & Herbs"	1/2 cup honey
1/2 cup cornmeal	1/2 cup safflower oil
1 finely chopped green	1 to 3 eggs
pepper	1 can mushroom soup
1 can creamed corn	and/or chopped
1/4 tsp baking soda	mushrooms

HOLIDAY DRESSING

This can be stuffed into a chicken, turkey, squash, or served by itself.

1 cup diced apples	2 cups dried bread
2 cups crumbled	crumbs
cornbread	1/4 tsp Cornucopia "All
1/4 to 1/2 cup pinoli nuts	Spices and Herbs"

1 cup diced celery	1 cup tree chestnuts
1 diced green pepper	or water chestnuts

Mix thoroughly, stuff and bake in oven. If stuffing in a bird, the following preparations are recommended: Soak the bird overnight in 1/4 cup of salt per 1/2 gallon distilled water. Rinse thoroughly in fresh water then bring to a boil or just before. Notice the debris floating to the top. Rinse thoroughly. Baste inside and out with a mixture of 1 tsp thyme, 1 to 2 drops of mint and sufficient olive oil. Stuff with Holiday Dressing and bake.

GRITS

Soak about 24 hours in distilled water. Start with 3 to 3-1/2 cups of water per cup of grits. They will need to be cooked at least 2 hours or until they are creamy. Start with the following ingredients:

2 cups white corn grits	1/2 tbsp salt (optional)
1/4 cup safflower oil	1/8 cup honey
1/2 tsp molasses	1/2 tbsp teriyaki
1/4 tsp Cornucopia "All Spices and Herbs"	1/2 to 1 can of creamed corn

Add creamed corn after one hour of cooking.
Stir regularly and add water as needed to maintain
creamy state.

FRENCH STYLE GRITS

Pour cooked grits onto a sheet cake pan and spread out evenly. Put into the refrigerator overnight. The next morning, cut the solidified grits into 3 inch squares and dip into the following dip, fry in frying pan with corn oil, and serve as is or with syrup or whatever suits your taste. Enough flour and cornmeal in a one-to-one ratio to thicken. Will dip 2 pounds grits.

6 eggs	1/4 large chopped onion (fine)
1 tbsp honey	1/2 tsp molasses
pinch of Cornucopia "All Spices and Herbs"	1/2 tbsp relish
1/2 tsp salt (optional)	1/4 tsp Worchestershire sauce
pinch of paprika	

RAW KEY LIME PIE

Crust:

2 cups of macadamia nuts soaked overnight in purified water — one can additionally rinse with a tablespoon of 35 percent food grade hydrogen peroxide to kill any fungus on the nuts. Be careful not to spill the peroxide in your hands. If you do, rinse profusely with water.

Add to the soaked nuts (one could use cashews, pecans, or skinned almonds) a half cup of shredded coconut and 6 soaked dates. Put this in a food processor until well puréed. This mix is then pressed into a glass pie pan.

Filling:

Put 2 to 4 ripe avocados into the food processor or blender until creamy. Add the juice of 10 to 12 fresh-squeezed limes and sweeten to taste with stevia, Truvia, Ki-Sweet, maple syrup, xylitol, or whatever sweetener is your preference. Pour this into the pie crust and place into the freezer for 45 to 60 minutes to until the pie is solidified. Cut and serve cold. You could dress up the pie a bit with sliced pecans placed on top.

The same mix can be used to make chocolate mousse pie by using organic cocoa powder rather than the lime juice. Both pies are nutritious, delicious and easy to make.

There are thousands of excellent recipes and methods of preparing food. Use those that best suit your tastes and needs. Remember, the higher the natural quality of any food, the better it tastes and the fewer condiments necessary to make it palatable.

Sally Fallon of the Weston A. Price Foundation has a delightful book called *Nourishing Traditions* that may be helpful. Regardless of what dietary program you choose to follow, high-Brix whole foods are a mandatory part of that dietary program. Research over the past twenty years points to a low-glycemic diet as depicted by Cenegenics and discussed in the book *The Life Plan* by Jeffry Life, MD, as being most healthy, whether vegetarian or not. A low-glycemic diet means no white flours, sugars, or grains such as white rice. Actually, most people would be much healthier if they eliminated grains completely from their diets. Grains are not needed for people to be healthy, contrary to what the USDA contends. The book *Wheat Belly*, by William Davis, MD, is an excellent elaboration on that subject specific to wheat.

Here are some helpful, healthful hints you may choose to adopt. When a sweetener, particularly white sugar, is called for or desired, use Stevia, honey, KiSweet, Amazon Naturals or fresh fruit juice. If you insist upon sugar then use organic cane juice or evaporated cane juice. Non-organic sugar cane is sprayed with glyphosate prior to harvest so buy only "organic" cane sugar. Beet sugar is genetically engineered and sprayed with glyphosate, so avoid completely.

Blue corn is best as it has additional phyto-nutrients over yellow or white corn all else equal. Buy only organic or verified non-GMO corn products, otherwise they will be genetically modified. In any event, select the corn with the highest Brix reading.

Select sugar cane molasses over beet molasses. The mineral content and palatability of the sugar cane molasses are usually better.

When canning fruits and vegetables, first juice some of the produce to use as the canning liquid rather than adding any water. You'll be pleased with the results.

Use molasses and herbs liberally as condiments to increase the spectrum of nutrients in the food.

If you eat meat, it is greatly beneficial to first soak the meat in 1/4 cup of non-iodized salt per 1/2 gallon distilled water for twelve hours (two hours for hamburger). After soaking, rinse two or three times with distilled water and after the last rinsing leave the meat in the water and bring the water just to a boil. Agitate the water slightly, dump, and rinse once more. You will notice the great amount of off-color material and debris that comes out of the meat. This detritus is not conducive to health. The meat is now ready to be cooked or prepared as usual. If well-prepared, you will notice a sharp improvement over unclean meat.

Stay alert to practices that follow biological reasons and improve your health, vitality, and attitude.

Unfortunately, in 2014, many of the statements I made originally in 1989 are no longer absolute. Dr. Carey Reams believed that corn oil was a great product for people to consume. That is not the case in my opinion. Even if he were correct about this belief in the 1950s and 1960s, it is not correct today. Corn oil comes from genetically engineered corn, and, as we have found via

Weston A. Price and others, we are much better off to consume coconut oil, olive oil, macadamia nut oil, and organic butter rather than corn oil.

Sugar beets today are genetically engineered and sprayed with glyphosate. Sugar cane is sprayed with glyphosate before harvest. Neither sugar is clean anymore.

A thorough overview of these and many other food issues is explained in my book *Food Plague*. Please read it for the latest on what is happening to our food chain and food quality.

Chapter 9

Technology on the Horizon

It is said that planet Earth is in the midst of an information explosion. Computers, robots, and fiber optics are commonplace. Despite all of man's fabulous technology, and also as a result of it, he has created an environmental situation that teeters on the cutting edge of destruction. He has missed the most obvious phenomenon of all: there is no phenomenon that man has invented or made use of that is not already found in nature. The sophisticated antennae of space age technology can be found on certain insects. The sophisticated navigation systems used by airplanes are surpassed by migrating animals and birds. The phenomenal and sometimes atrocious architecture of modern man is put to shame by ancient civilizations and far exceeded in beauty by nature herself.

Man brags about new genetic strains of crops that resist diseases and insects, bring higher yields, and are better all-around because of man's ingenuity. Man has been on an ego trip for a long time. The new technology on the horizon is man's cooperative progression with nature herself. Nature has the capacity to produce perfect crops that are completely disease and insect free, do not rot, yield far beyond man's wildest expectations, need no rescue chemicals or preservatives, and are perfectly mineralized.

An operation that grows plants from seed to harvest in just a few hours will be perfected and the complete revitalization in a single growing season of sterilized soils and deserts will be unfolded — both *completely without* the slightest need for toxic chemicals. The latter is pretty well established fact. Additionally, electromagnetic instruments to control insects like mosquitoes and flies will be commercialized.

What is the presence in 2014 of these last two claims from edition one? Thanks to Advancing Eco-Agriculture, a grower in central Indiana, in the midst of the 2012 drought where neighbors' crops were literally dried up and dead, an organic farmer grew 170 bushel per acre of blue corn. The previous best for the area had been seventy-five bushels of organic blue corn per acre.

Entomologist Tom Dykstra, PhD, a protégé of Dr. Phil Callahan, has devised an insect trap based upon the principles of Dr. Callahan's electromagnetic theories for insect communication. This trap is available at www.dykstralabs.com.

There are many things the average farmer or layman can do to advance this technology. First, get out of the rut, whether it is junk food twenty-one times per week or the "natural all-organic" movement. All organic is great, but without mineralization it is no better than chemical. The technology of the future involves biological measurements not just physical and chemical measurements. Everything emits an energy field. Dr. Philip Callahan has proved that insects communicate and find food using these energy emissions. Each species of life has its unique whole frequency that comprises an infinite number of component frequencies. When these energies are properly evaluated, it is possible and practical to set optimum conditions for growth and proliferation according to natural laws, not man-made standards. Often man's physical observations are made through such a narrow lens that the true picture remains unseen. When subtle biological energies are evaluated, a more complete picture emerges, and thus a more progressive plan of action can be made. Tesla was able to tap into some of these energies to produce "free" electrical power at the turn of the century. He was ahead of his time, and his inventions were suppressed. The tide has turned in favor of progressive coexistence rather than accelerating demise. Learn about the subtle biological energies, use them to grow healthful food, and rest assured this planet will be inhabitable for your progeny.

NICE-TO-KNOW INFORMATION

Bark splitting. Bark splitting on trees is due to a plugged vascular system. It is caused sequentially by the following nutrient deficiencies: calcium, phosphate, selenium, cobalt/copper. Sul-Po-Mag applied between July 15 and September 15 acts as a cathartic (laxative) for the vascular system but it is only a symptomatic correction and the nutrient deficiencies must be corrected to solve the problem.

Dandelions. Dandelions are a common weed in lawns and fields. They are a red-light signal of the following sequential nutrient deficiencies: calcium, phosphate, vitamin A, iron. Correct these deficiencies, and dandelions will disappear.

Nature has a wondrous way of talking to us. When a nutrient deficiency first begins to manifest itself at a low level, the bacteria arrive on the scene. This can be termed a first-degree deficiency. As the deficiency worsens, at a certain point the fungi show up. This can be termed a second-degree deficiency. The third-degree level attracts the viruses and the fourth-degree level attracts the insects and parasites.

Afterword

The saying goes that time is only relative. Your experience of time is measured by your action or inaction. This is a time for action. Every individual is personally responsible, and no one is an island. Improve the quality of your food now and your health, vitality, and attitude will improve along with it. If you can only obtain produce from the local grocer, then select the best and regularly request better quality and greater variety. If you can grow produce yourself, do so. If you can only add condiments to change the quality, do so. All citizens can write to their congressman and demand that government learning institutions research and teach quality fertilization and nondestructive agricultural practices.

This is everyone's country. Find out why this government proclaims we have a glut of agricultural commodities, and yet imports more than it exports of many of these commodities. Find out why the government will not allow farmers to export commodities directly when foreign buyers beg for the commodities and offer much higher prices for them. Find out why our government has sold millions of tons per year of our phosphate to Russia when they have a much larger and more accessible phosphate reserve. Find out why the government allows thousands of acres per day of the South American rainforests to be stripped for grazing beef cattle that are imported to this country and labeled domestic beef. Find out why the government suppresses the development and marketing of non-polluting free energy machines. This is still the greatest country in the world. Only enlightened action toward the implementation of free energy usage and high-quality, nondestructive food production will keep it that way. You may hear the principles presented in this book rebutted with the statement, ". . . if these are so good and correct, why doesn't everyone practice them?" Education is good, too, so why doesn't everyone get it?

You probably notice that the following statistics from the first edition of this book quite drastically contradict the propaganda repeatedly broadcast by the news media which is that the American farmer produces enough food for the entire world and that this country possesses tremendous surpluses. There are two motives behind this propaganda. One is for control, manipulation, profit, and possession of the land. When the farm is broke, the government takes the land. Private ownership of the land is the foundation of democracy. The other motive is a cover-up. The powers that be do not want the general public to learn of the serious degenerative status of the soils in this country. If the public knew, changes would occur.

Appendix

Parity pricing is something farmers like to point to in order to contend that they are or are not receiving their fair share of market prices. This is a term based upon the 1910–1914 prices received compared to cost of production for that same time. One hundred means the two equal. Farmers have long contended that they should receive parity pricing, and in fact the farm bills usually have some type of subsidy program to help with the prices farmers receive versus the market price to move the farmers revenues closer to "parity" at taxpayers' expense. The current price for slaughter beef cattle as of April 2, 2013, averaged $126 per hundred weight.[1] Parity price per USDA economists is about $292 per hundred weight. Fluid milk is about $18 per hundred weight while parity is $52. Corn is just under $7.00 per bushel while parity price is about $12 per bushel.[2]

Foods produced today are much different than those in 1910–1914. Today they have significantly less mineral and are contaminated with antibiotics, growth hormones, herbicides and pesticides, mycotoxins, genetically engineered proteins, and resistant

---

[1] "Five Area Monthly Weighted Average Direct Slaughter Cattle — Negotiated," USDA Market News Service, February 10, 2014, http://www.ams.usda.gov/mnreports/lm_ct180.txt.
[2] Stu Ellis, "Are You Ready for Production Quotas and Parity Prices in Agriculture?," FarmGateBlog.com, December 25, 2012, http://www.farmgateblog.com/article/1716/are-you-ready-for-production-quotas-and-parity-prices-in-agriculture.

pathogens. The cost of these "foods" to society is significant when considering the medical care costs that must be expended because of these adultered foods today. Farmers that produce real food have no problems getting paid parity or above pricing whether it be for organic grass-fed beef, A2 raw milk, or high-Brix organic tree fruit.

Looking at the older data provided from edition one of this book, the only consistent occurrence in the past 20 years is further degradation of the food coming off the farm via continued demineralization, genetic engineering, and pesticide/drug use.

According to the USDA Foresight Agricultural Service, the United States for 2012–2013 produced 286,005,000 metric tons of course grains and consumed 277,114,000 metric tons for the same period.[1]

Adding to these figures 61,755,000 metric tons of wheat production and 38,109,000 metric tons of wheat consumption yields 347,760,000 metric tons production and 315,223,000 metric tons of consumption of wheat and coarse grains. This equates to a 13.06 percent increase in production from 1984–1985 and a 6.93 percent increase in consumption from that same period.[2]

Milk production for 2012 was 200.3 billion pounds. Milk consumption/disappearance was 193.6 billion pounds.[3]

As one can see from the 1974 to 1984 data, U.S. milk production has increased to cover consumption.

The mantra that is repeated over and over by the media, government groups, environmental groups, the bio-tech industry, and its university mouthpieces is that we must have bio-technology in order to feed the ever-expanding world population. Just follow the money because that is a false statement. Per Don Huber and others, farmers only produce about 10 to 15 percent of the production potential of present, non-genetically engineered crop varieties. This

---

[1] "World's Coarse Grains Production, Consumption, and Stocks," USDA, February 10, 2014, http://www.fas.usda.gov/psdonline/psdreport.aspx?hidReportRetrievalName=BVS&hidReportRetrievalID=690&hidReportRetrievalTemplateID=7.
[2] National Agriculture Statistics Service, "Parity Prices, Parity Ratio, and Feed Price Ratio," USDA, http://www.nass.usda.gov/Surveys/Guide_to_NASS_Surveys/Prices/Chapter%20Four%20Parity%20and%20Feed%20Price%20Ratios%20v10.pdf.
[3] Jerry Cessna, "Situation and Outlook for the U.S. Dairy Industry," Agricultural Outlook Forum, February 22, 2013, http://www.usda.gov/oce/forum/presentations/DairyOutlook.pdf.

Table 4.1. Parity Ratio and Adjusted Parity Ratio by Year

Year	Parity Ratio %	Adjusted Parity Ratio %	Year	Parity Ratio %	Adjusted Parity Ratio %
1959	81	82	1985	52	55
1960	80	82	1986	51	56
1961	79	83	1987	51	58
1962	80	83	1988	54	60
1963	78	81	1989	55	59
1964	76	80	1990	50	53
1965	76	81	1991	47	50
1966	79	85	1992	47	49
1967	73	79	1993	47	50
1968	73	79	1994	45	47
1969	73	79	1995	44	46
1970	72	77	1996	47	48
1971	70	75	1997	43	45
1972	74	79	1998	42	45
1973	91	94	1999		
1974	86	87	2000	39	43
1975	76	76	2001	40	44
1976	71	72	2002	38	40
1977	66	68	2003	40	43
1978	70	72	2004	42	44
1979	71	72	2005	38	42
1980	65	65	2006	37	39
1981	60	62	2007	40	42
1982	55	57	2008	39	40
1983	56	57	2009	35	36
1984	58	59	2010	38	39

Computed using indexes on the 1910-14 = 100 base period. The parity ratios are also available for each year 1910-1958

shortfall is not an issue of genetics or genetic manipulation. It is a matter of nutrition and soil fertility management.

Our current crops have the capacity for 500 bushel corn, 200 bushel soybeans, 300 bushel wheat, and so forth. Read the book, *Epigenetics: How Environment Shapes our Genes* by Richard C. Francis. It's not crop genetics that are holding us back; it's farm management, specifically the lack of farm nutritional management.

Please read my other books for more information on how we can solve these many problems. May your quest be fruitful and your successes on the farm and in the garden many.

Percentage of Beef Graded, 1984, From U.S.D.A. Source

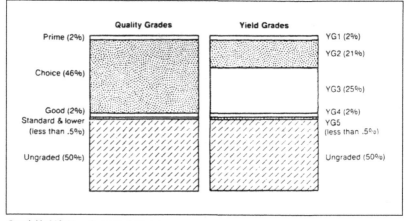

Compiled by Mike Toner, Stuarts Draft, Virginia.
Facsimile reproduction from page 23, Acres U.S.A., September 1986.

U.S. MILK PRODUCTION AND USAGE
(in billion pounds)

YEAR	CONSUMPTION	PRODUCTION	DIFFERENCE	IMPORTS
1974	119.5	115.6	(3.9)	2.9
1975	120.6	115.4	(5.2)	1.7
1976	121.7	120.2	(1.5)	1.9
1977	122.9	122.7	(0.2)	2.0
1978	124.8	121.5	(3.3)	2.3
1980	127.0	128.4	1.4	2.1
1981	130.4	132.8	2.4	2.3
1982	136.5	135.5	(6.3)	2.7
1983	138.7	139.7	1.0	2.6
1984	141.7	135.4	(6.3)	2.7
Total	1,410.6	1,390.6	(20.0)	25.3

Average for 11 years—(1.82) Billion Pounds

Consumption includes actual military donation and actual on-farm usage.

These figures come from *Dairy Outlook and Situation Year Book,* DS 401, Pages 28 and 34.

Note: The figures encased in parentheses have a minus value.

USE GREATER THAN PRODUCTION
U.S. Wheat and Coarse Grains (Million Metric Tons)

YEAR	BEGINNING STOCKS	PRODUCTION	TOTAL USE	IMPORTS	ENDING STOCKS	USE AS % OF PRODUCTION
60/61	105.6	178.8	166.7	0.6	118.3	93%
61/62	118.3	161.0	175.5	0.5	104.3	100%
62/63	104/3	159.3	170.8	0.3	93.2	107%
63/64	93.2	171.5	175.0	0.4	90.1	102%
64/65	90.1	157.5	172.9	0.4	76.5	109%
65/66	76.5	179.1	197.8	0.3	58.2	110%
66/67	58.2	180.7	189.7	0.3	49.5	104%
67/68	49.5	203.9	191.0	0.3	62.7	93%
68/69	62.7	197.6	188.9	0.3	71.8	95%
70/71	72.8	182.9	201.6	0.4	54.6	110%
71/72	54.6	233.6	215.1	0.4	73.4	92%
72/73	73.4	224.1	250.0	0.5	48.0	111%
73/74	48.0	233.3	250.5	0.3	31.1	107%
74/75	31.1	199.4	203.7	0.6	27.3	102%
75/76	27.3	243.3	235.7	0.5	35.5	96%
76/77	35.5	252.8	228.4	0.4	60.3	90%
77/78	60.3	261.4	248.6	0.4	73.5	95%
78/79	73.5	270.5	272.7	0.3	71.6	100%
79/80	71.6	296.5	291.2	0.4	77.2	98%
80/81	77.2	263.1	279.1	0.3	61.6	106%
81/82	61.6	322.4	244.6	0.4	99.8	88%
82/83	99.8	326.0	287.7	0.6	138.7	88%
83/84	138.7	203.0	272.7	0.8	69.8	134%
84/85	69.8	307.6	294.8	0.9	83.5	95%
25 years		5610.3	5645.1	11.0		

Notes: Coarse grains include corn, sorghum, barley, oats, and rye. Average Annual Production-224.4 Million Ton. Average Annual Total Use-225.8 Million Ton. Total usage of wheat and coarse grain is greater than total production for this 25 year period. Total use is 100.6% of total production. These figures do not represent a surplus! They show government supply management. The same necessary pipeline inventory and reserve accumulated from all past years is used to keep grain cheap. Ending stocks are less than in the early 1960s even though annual usage has increased 76%. Ending stocks as a percent of annual use has dropped form 71% to 28% in 1985. Source: USDA, World Grain Situation and Outlook, February 12, 1985.

BEEF FACTS ANALYSIS . . . *by Mike Toner & Harold D. Beyeller*

Applied Use	Domestic Beef Production (million lbs.) [Agr. Statistics USDA 1984 Pg. 310 Tab 455]	Domestic Beef Consumption (million lbs.) [Agr. Statistics USDA 1984 Pg. 310 Tab 455]	Domestic Production for Military Consumption (million lbs.) [Food Consumption Bulletin #736 Pg. 47 Tab 34A]	Domestic Beef Production for U.S. Territories (million lbs.) [Agr. Statistics USDA 1984 Pg. 311 Tab 456]	Shortage of U.S. Beef Production Cols. 2-3-4 compared to col. 1 (million lbs) [Summary Columns 1-2-3-4]	Beef Exports to Foreign Countries (million lbs.) [Agr. Statistics USDA 1984 Pg. 311 Tab 456]	Imports of Foreign Beef (million lbs.) [Food Consumption Bulletin #736 Pg. 47 Tab 34A Average of 4 Bulletins USDA]	Live Beef Animals Imported Under 200 lb. (No. animals) [FATUS Economic Research USDA 1984 Pg. 139]	Live Beef Animals Imported 200 to 699 lbs. (No. animals) [FATUS Economic Research USDA 1984 Pg. 139]	Live Beef Animals Imported over 700 lbs. (No. Animals) [FATUS Economic Research USDA 1984 Pg. 139]	Total Animals Per Year (No. Animals) [These Animals show up in our Domestic Beef Production Column #1]
	1	2	3	4	5	6	7	8	9	10	11
1970	21685	22926	465	65	1791	40	1792	168933	906992	66,975	1,142,900
1971	21904	23086	407	68	1657	53	1734	158689	748873	61,523	969,085
1972	22413	23956	302	62	1907	62	1960	173336	939168	56,531	1,169,035
1973	21278	22814	229	61	1826	91	1990	143851	783851	95,742	1,023,444
1974	23137	24488	195	67	1613	63	1615	77602	413777	64,810	556,189
1975	23975	25397	278	71	1771	54	1758	10145	220651	151,932	382,928
1976	25969	27539	231	80	1881	90	2073	119814	562707	290,098	972,619
1977	25279	27048	151	78	1998	103	1939	133067	731247	263,325	1,127,639
1978	24241	25998	237	58	2052	163	2297	154972	873542	214,548	1,243,062
1979	21477	23522	170	51	2266	170	2405	146133	430726	144,095	720,954
1980	21643	23320	189	48	1914	176	2064	135937	382325	154,004	672,266
1981	22389	23756	195	37	1599	221	1743	145653	370056	135,295	651,004
1982	22536	23998	135	57	1654	254	1939	159606	605768	231,379	996,753
1983	23243	24710	121	41	1629	272	1931	88564	587669	235,082	911,315
1984	23598	24900	112	47	1461	328	1823	77845	406921	262,180	746,946
1985	23728	25331	126	51	1780	328	2068	34749	573368	221,601	829,718

Acres U.S.A., September 1986, page 23.

Bibliography

Callahan, Philip A. *Ancient Mysteries, Modern Visions: The Magnetic Life of Agriculture*. Kansas City, MO: Acres U.S.A., 1984.

Callahan, Philip A. *Tuning in to Nature: Solar Energy, Infrared Radiation, and the Insect Communication System*. Greenwich, CT: The Devin-Adair Co., 1975. Republished by Acres U.S.A.

Janick, Jules, Robert W. Schery, Frank W. Woods, and Vernon W. Ruttan. *Plant Science: An Introduction to World Crops*. San Francisco: W. H. Freeman and Company, 1974.

Nieper, Hans A. *Dr. Nieper's Revolution in Technology, Medicine and Society: Conversion of Gravity Field Energy*. Oldenburg, Germany: Druckhaus Neue Stalling, 1985.

Skow, Dan, and Derrice Skow. *Food for Thought*. Fairmont, Minnesota, 1983.

Walters, Charles, Jr., ed. *Acres, U.S.A.* Volumes 1–18. Kansas City, Missouri, 1971–1988.

Index

pH, 12, 30, 32; as nutrient indicator, 79–80; in soil, 26–27
phosphate, 11, 16–17, 67; and disease prevention, 79–80; in relation to photosynthesis, 24; shortage, 42–43; sources of, 16–17
phosphorus, 16–17
photosynthesis, 3, 23–24, 43
pollution, xi, xiii, 46, 83
potash, 17–19, 29–30, 31, 66–67; deficiency, 43, 44, 80; sources of, 17–18, 68. *See also* muriate of potash
potassium, 17–18
potassium chloride, 37–38, 39, 43
potato, 50, 72; disorders of, 22, 74, 90; planter, 67
potting soil, recipes for, 63–65
pumpkin, 72; disorders of, 77

radionics, ix–x
raspberries, 72; disorders of, 75–76
Reams, Carey, 6, 13, 32, 58, 103
refractive index, 86, 90–94
refractometer, 30, 43, 62; use of, 86–90
Reich, Wilhelm, 2, 3, 5
remineralization, of soil, 10
Rescue Remedy, 65
respiration, 24
rhizobium nodules, 29
RNA, 16
Robertson, H. H., 6
roots, dip for, 65
roses, 71; disorders of, 76

salt, buildup in soil, 15, 41, 45–46, 51, 55
Science, 6
seaweed products, 22, 61–62
Seed Soak, 64–65
seeds, mineral content test, 64
Seike, Shirrichi, 1
selenium, 41, 81
single-nutrient fix, 42, 43, 46–47
Skow, Dan, 32, 40
soil, 9; and calcium, 14; and carbon, 20; and salt buildup, 45–46; balances, 54–56; chemistry, elements of, 10–11; degradation of, 36–37; electronic scanner testing, 34–35; Le Motte testing equipment, 32–34; preparation

for garden, 57–61; quality of, 32; test reports, 26–36; testing of, 25–44; testing report and recommendations, 29–32; worthwhile testing, 32
squash, 72; disorders of, 77
Statistical Abstract of the U.S. 1985, xiv
stilbestrol, 96
strawberries, 66, 71–72; disorders of, 77
sugar, addiction to, 23; in plants, 16, 19, 45, 88
Sulfa ammonis, 21
sunlight, 2–3, 4, 63

Temik, 82
Tesla function, 6
Tesla, Nikola, x, 2, 106
tilling, 59–60, 62–63, 66
tissue test, 36, 58, 71
tomato, 19, 65; insects and disorder of, 73–74
topsoil, xi, xiii,7, 32, 34
transmutative energy, 6, 70–71

University of Florida, 50
urea, 67, 68
USDA, xi, 102, 111, 112

velvet leaf. *See* buttonweed
vibration, frequency of, 50
virus,70, 107
vitamin C, 81

weeds, 21, 51–55, 60, 85

zinc, 54

Acres U.S.A. — books are just the beginning!

Farmers and gardeners around the world are learning to grow bountiful crops profitably—without risking their own health and destroying the fertility of the soil. *Acres U.S.A.* can show you how. If you want to be on the cutting edge of organic and sustainable growing technologies, techniques, markets, news, analysis and trends, look to *Acres U.S.A.* For 40 years, we've been the independent voice for eco-agriculture. Each monthly issue is packed with practical, hands-on information you can put to work on your farm, bringing solutions to your most pressing problems. Get the advice consultants charge thousands for . . .

- Fertility management
- Non-chemical weed & insect control
- Specialty crops & marketing
- Grazing, composting, natural veterinary care
- Soil's link to human & animal health

For a free sample copy or to subscribe, visit us online at

www.acresusa.com

or call toll-free in the U.S. and Canada

1-800-355-5313

Outside U.S. & Canada call 970-392-4464

• info@acresusa.com